To Ma  *ove*

*Poems ~~~~ ~~~
from the Pembrokeshire coast
by Christopher Jessop*

*Illustrated throughout
Music scored for piano*

Springboard Press

Published in 2016
by
Springboard Press
1 West End Marloes via Haverfordwest Pembrokeshire
West Wales
SA62 3BE
United Kingdom

www.asummerbreak.co.uk

ISBN 978 0 9928774 1 5

A CIP record for this title is available from The British Library.

Disclaimer
This is a work of fiction. Names, characters, businesses, organisations, places, events and incidents are either the products of the author's imagination or are used in a completely fictitious manner. Any resemblance to actual persons, living or dead, or actual events is purely coincidental.

Typeset in Perpetua 12 on 14 point

Printed and bound in Wales at
Gomer Press, Llandysul, Ceredigion

Dear Reader

Here are many stories, told in verse, which take you through the year. There are tales about Nature and wildlife, adventures set in the countryside and on the Pembrokeshire coast, dreams of people both exploring in boats and diving under the waves...

All these stories can be read as poems; I have composed original tunes for most of those which also work well as songs.

I hope you like the pictures in this book; some should help to set the scene, while others pick up particular details in poems or songs.

Whenever you read a poem out loud or sing a song, you bring those words to life in your own special way –
But your inventiveness needn't stop there.

Inspired by its stories, why not make this whole book something unique? Giving your imagination free rein, use colour to transform all of my black and white sketches...

...And so create a lively pocket gallery of your own pictures, illustrated in words by my poems and songs!

Wishing you much enjoyment

Christopher Jessop

Acknowledgements

All credit to Mary Inder, for suggesting that I should publish an illustrated collection of my poems and songs; crucially, Mary very kindly agreed to act as my editor.

Robin Black's sound recording work was invaluable; I am greatly indebted to Dale Amateur Dramatic Society's Head of Music, who interpreted and transcribed my scribbles and awful noises to produce musical scores, and to Anne Meeke, who "test drove" the various drafts on her kindly piano.

For their enduring encouragement my thanks to Dave Paley, Penny, Amelia and Ryan Bird, Sophy Cullington, Rosemary Royle, Caroline Walmsley, and Christiania Whitehead. Also I must remember Shelagh Alvarez, the remarkable lady who founded the Peninsula Poets group, and much-missed Jean Thomas who so enlivened our every gathering in Dale.

It is as true for these songs and poems as it was for my first novel, **A Summer Break**: the Pembrokeshire coast has constantly inspired me. So, this book is my way of thanking Nature – not just for her magnificent sweeping bays and soaring rugged cliffs, but for the little-known paths and secret coves and inlets... Where rare flowers can flourish, unnoticed except by the insects that depend on them; and wild creatures may come close, less afraid of quiet and respectful humans.

You will find musical scores for all of the song tunes composed by me at the end of the book, just ahead of the index. With one exception they are scored for piano, but here's hoping that the tunes will get to be played on all sorts of instruments...

Because no score is particularly easy to read when it has been reduced to fit on the pages of a book this size, the scores are available free of charge via the Springboard Press website,

www.asummerbreak.co.uk.

Using the "Contact Us" section, you can request the scores as digital files: you will be emailed .jpeg images, which you can print out at any size you wish.

To Marloes, With Love

Christopher Jessop

TO MARLOES, WITH LOVE

To Marloes, with Love,
As a child you first came…
Nowhere else on this Earth
Makes you feel quite the same.

To Marloes with Love, so much love for The Sea:
The beautiful, secretive, playworthy Sea,
The everso-swimmable, dangerous, life-giving Sea!

To Marloes with Love, silent love for The Sky.
Its horizon so wide and its blue depth so high…
They small you to nothing, then let your thoughts fly.

To Marloes with Love,
And a craving for Truth:
It thrives in wild places, hides behind human faces.

To Marloes with Love,
Fired by passion for Art:
Depict what you truly feel, write from your heart!

To Marloes, all nerves,
With a newly-made friend…
Will they see the beauty? On this, much depends.

To Marloes, with Love and now children you come:
Let them go wild and free in the Sea and the Sun!

To Marloes with Love,
On and on down the years…
The wisdom of Nature shows ever more clear.

From Marloes, With Love, to the rest of the World:
A gift we can never name, worth more than gold.

CHRISTMAS DAY IS NEARLY HERE

Christmas Day is nearly here: the lights shine on the tree,
And underneath sit presents, some for you and some for me.
We've hung the mistletoe up, and the ivy and the holly;
Tinsel glitters, baubles shine, and everywhere looks jolly.

Christmas Day is nearly here: so much food is in the house
That our cat patrols with extra care, on watch for Mister Mouse.
The cake was finished weeks ago,
The pudding just needs steaming;
The sideboard's piled with fruit and nuts
Which set our eyes a-gleaming.

Christmas Day is nearly here:
The folks are coming home.
Uncle's 'plane will soon be boarding
At the airport, there in Rome,
And Big Sister's train at Paddington
Is ready to depart;
As they journey ever closer, we'll get such jumpy hearts.

Christmas Day is nearly here –
And, oh, how time does seem to drag!
So out we go, in coats and scarves,
To play with next door's dog.
It takes us off across the fields, then to the shore we run:
It knows that sea-smoothed low tide beach
Is the perfect place for fun!

Christmas Day is nearly here, and out in Sandy Haven bay
Lie merchant ships which normally would hurry on their way;
But the forecast was quite stormy, so it made their skippers say,
'Let's stay here, good and sheltered,
For a peaceful Christmas Day.'

Christmas Day is nearly here: when we come back from the beach
We meet some other children at the swings and football pitch;
And because it's almost Christmas, our greetings are so friendly –
Even for that sneaky Simon, and his bighead sister Wendy!

Christmas Day is nearly here, and the basket's full of wood;
The logs burn well, the fire is bright, the heat it feels so good.
We sit around it glowing,
Now we've bathed and washed our hair…
And left upstairs really steamy, talcum powder everywhere!

Christmas Day is nearly here, and now everyone's arrived:
Mum bustles yet more madly, Gran is really misty-eyed.
Uncle tells us tales of Italy, but his jokes get Dad confused;
Pussy cuddles with Big Sister, to quietly learn her news.

Christmas Day is nearly here: see our socks, all hung up high;
We played a game, and then came time for cocoa and mince pies.
With minty teeth and hair well brushed,
To bed we now must go…
As we snuggle down and close our eyes, outside it starts to snow.

A SNOWFALL ON THE COAST

For winter after winter, the only sight of snow that Pembrokeshire coast-dwellers enjoy is a glimpse of the Presceli tops thinly whitened for a short while – perhaps a day or two.

So, when it comes, a proper covering right on the sea's margin is not to be wasted.

The morning is so quiet; outside, the air's quite still –
And, now, I realise: no sound of cars at all!
Our bedroom's really chilly: my breath white-clouds the air,
And there leaks around our curtains a truly glacial glare...
As, shivering, I peep through them, I already know:
A rosy sun is rising on a West Wales deep in snow.

The sky stretches ever bluer above a scene all white;
I gasp to see how deep the drifts: 'It must have snowed all night!'
Downstairs I rouse the kitchen's stove, and admit an urgent cat;
With proud miaows she shows me – one doorstep, two dead rats.
The all-night-simmered kettle only needs a tad more heat;
Soon I take up tea and biscuits: your winter weekend treat.

Before you dress to start the day we snuggle, changing plans:
No going shopping in your car, no oil-change for my van;
Instead, two young folk still asleep need help to make the most
Of this rarity in Pembrokeshire: a snowfall on the coast.
So, while with spices and dried fruit ~
You make us special porridge,
I'll have to go a-hunting: where, in which shed, my old sledge?

A silent snowy morning, all sparkling in the sun.
A perfect snowy morning; Nature wants us to have fun,
And it's perfect snow, this morning: oh, how that sledge will run!
A heavily snowy morning, the land iced like a cake:
A beautiful cold morning, many photographs to take.
A silent snowy morning – until the children wake!

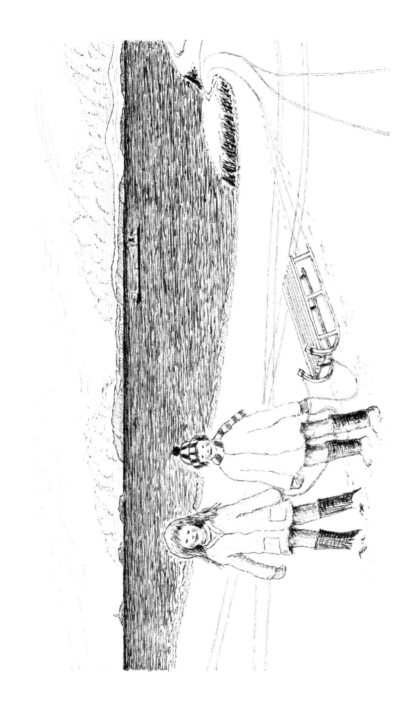

NEW YEAR'S DAY

The sky is a crow-scattered driving greyness;
To the evident delight of scores of ducks,
Tufted bums up-tilting as dredging bills dip down,
Marloes Mere is brimmed to its boundary bulwarks.

Laning through the sedge,
And then wind-leaning up the coastward track across the bare ley,
We reach the gust-shuddered gate, and clat through
Onto the cliff path…

And there it is: the New Year Atlantic.
Grey-green, but topped with plenty of truculent white.

Departing Saint Anne's, a laden tanker
Stubs its westbound bow against the weather's heavy sidekicks:
We picture a spray-peering watchkeeper,
Wheel-nimble their helming,
Whose legs subconsciously adjust to every tilt and dip
Of a wiper-smeared horizon.

His – or her – ears will meanwhile be vigilant
For engine mis-beats; and, of course, electronic alerts
From any of those almost over-informative screens
Which seem to lay siege
To any ship's steering position, these days:
They, which tell so much yet actually know nothing –
For how can anything computerised
Ever have any *feel* for The Sea?

Let all be well: let that ship safely reach her Irish destination,
Bringing fresh fuel against the certainty
Of frost, these coming months,
Despite today's mildness.

Having watched our ship until she's
Comfortably beyond that untrustworthy tide race
With all its scheming gyres,
We turn for home, our heads now gratefully un-beered…

Rendered "gin-clear", indeed, we grinningly agree,
After a serious morning binge
On great draughts of ocean-fresh oxygen.

The New Year's sea lovingly greeted,
Our russeted cheeks dusted salty
By the spray-blown kisses of its bursting swell,
We glad our way back up the boot-grooved cliffside…

…And we are now so well-mooded, in fact,
That we only curse with chuckles
When the mud of last night's rain
Nearly slithers everyone prone –
And us, for a change, in quite smart clothes!

MISTER BLACK

A poem describing an individual from recent history, known to certain of us, who genuinely terrorised the Wild West... The Wild West of the Marloes peninsula, that is, not the American Wild West. Nevertheless, these verses do work best when read out loud in a loping cowboy drawl.

A bandy cat resides at Trehill Farm.

No, no: he's no domestic, this one –
No kitchen mat beside the Aga, his.
He's a clawslinger,
Goes ranging across the baking potato badlands;
When it rains, he holes up in Grainbin Gulch.

Who is he?
I don't know. All I can do is tell you what I do know.
About his appearance...
For sure, you'll know him if you see him.
He is the colour of night in a dark barn.
His coat is just a little bit dishevelled;
But then, like him, it ain't exactly new.

He only got one and a half ears,
On account of he had a dis-pute with a black back gull.
Now, after he had assured me
That that particular bird wouldn't ever harm no other cat,
I asked him, might he elaborate...?
Well – no. He just replied, 'Rabbit tastes better.'

He still got two eyes.
Both of them is the colour of broken beer bottles,
Shining in the sun
As they lays in the road outside the Lobster Pot Saloon,
The morning after a good quality fight.

As for the blacks of them eyes –
You'll never see nothing blacker unless
You goes down into Hell
And sweeps out the soot from the chimneys of Satan's furnaces!

His claws? Like cut-throat razors:
'Had them sharpened jist today!'

Don't have no name.
Never given one, never needed one.
Because he don't answer to nobody.
But if you wants one to know him by –
Then MISTER BLACK will do.

He ain't no lawman: the only laws he recognises
Are those of Nature – and those that he invented for himself.
But rest assured:
For all that he's ignored,

For all his skulking, and his hiding,
And the way that, if you'se lucky enough to see him,
(Don't happen too often),
He'll look at you as if to say,
'WHAT THE HELL DO YOU WANT?' –
For all of that…
For downing outlaws, he's your man.

He ain't no pussy cat; he ain't no posse cat, neither.
This Cool-Paw Luke, this High Lanes Drifter
Does what he does well
Alone.
And I'm telling you:
He takes out
Low-down thieving banditos
Just any way he can.

He don't care if you're a dirty rat
Or, like many of 'em, fastidious clean.
He don't care.
He don't care: if you'se a rat he'll
Take you out –
Faster than a trap; and neater, too!

And if you,
Mister, Madam, Master, or Miss Mouse –
If you ventures outa your house at the wrong moment,
You ain't gonna be carin'
If you done forgot to lock the door.
Because you won't be coming back,
Once you've met with…

MISTER BLACK!

STING THE WIND

Sting the wind,
Wet the rain,
Bite the frost –
Walk again!

For I know, and the dog knows too:
Best time to walk is that hour of lowest tide,
When the stretching sand awaits us –
And also, brightly and whitely, the Moon tonight.

So – hat, coat, gloves, boots,
Lead.
No torch, this time:
No need.

And tomorrow…?

Though sting the wind,
Or wet the rain,
Or bite the frost –
We'll walk again!

Time to walk: it's the best time we know,
However the weather games its play.
Aye, always a good time, wherever we go…
Until Parson's Garden beckons, one day.

THE UP PLATFORM

A winter memory from my early years, when the family lived in Oxford; but Pembrokeshire folk of my age or older must have had similar experiences.

For another picture of a GWR Castle class loco, see Page 133.

Recalled always easily, my first meeting with that size of green:
Oh, what a sight! A presence so strong that I feel it now.
That easily-striding approach, frontally shining blue-black
Like a new-cleaned gun; with many steel pieces
Fresh-burnished to a knight's armour's brightness.

Growing in my oggling vision closer, and huger, then hugest;
Rolling in, ground-shuddering, until
– Only one stone slab away – it bafflingly obediently
Halts.
And is so tall above me, this face-warming Brunswick majesty,
Oil-tanned, sub-vibrant with thermodynamic agitation.

Its breath and scents, they swirl around:
Sweetness, slightly sulphur-stung –
Steam coal uniquely knows this scent's recipe.
Oleocaramel, and resinously rich fresh-from-overhaul paint;
Malty steam from copper pipe mouths purring.

Curlicue pops of fog wraith the flagstones now:
For a few seconds,
I and the other worshipping children
Are gaberdined angels
Floating with delight in their cloudy railway Heaven
Which is hot and damp,
And tastes of sleeper creosote, oil, and Horlicks.

Sizzling: the bright brass
Upturned bugle-mouthed bucket on its boiler's back.
Breathing, keen from its copperily cheerful chimney that's
Confident and heat-purpled in the watery morning sun,
And so deeply shiny,
And glinting so knowingly –
As a horse's eye does.

The bright black spokes of its wheels,
Which have carried it over the Avon watershed
And charioted down the sinuous Evenlode valley steels
From the cold Cotswolds:
These shine too, even in the gloom below the platform's edge.

All the sky's a-wobble
In the force of heat above its metal mouth.
Everything's syrup-rippled and jumpy:
The red and yellow signals
And the telegraph wires and their insulators
And the station starlings and the jet-trails.

"Watch out!" the fireman calls, and hauls the chain,
To swing out for his mate the swan-necked water crane
With its spattering elephantine trunk…
Now he's spun the valve wheel,
The loco's lion-emblemed tender
Rumbles profoundly as it fills.
Meanwhile, in the brake van behind it

The cart-and-cage-and-barrow men
Sling sacks,
Pass parcels,
And check the labels
Of basketed and livid cats
Whistling cheerfully all the while.

Above the poised ton knuckle of the connecting rod,
Avuncularly-lettered in noble brass
Within a gleaming, brass-framed arc,
Imperially grand – yet Christian named,
This mighty machine,
Even for the mere me…

SIR EDWARD ELGAR
(CASTLE CLASS)

"A Worcester engine," says Dad, "and that's appropriate".

And of course I don't know why; or what *appropriate* means.

Bolted to the cab-side, a brass-cast plate
Sports jolly-looking numbers in a portly script:
7 – 0 – 0 – 5.
It and all the other brightwork
Were Brasso'd before dawn at the shed.

And above the number,
Leaning from his cab in his grease-top cap,
Friendly and fag-lipped in his holey overalls,
A man whose job surely makes God jealous.

"Does the lad want to come up?"
And I, age of four but tall as seven,
Durst not –
But more from awe than fear.

For children should not stand
Where stands the better-than-Captain-or-Bishop-or-King, the
Man at the top of all achievement: the
DRIVER,
Master of two tons of fire,
Ninety of steel, and twenty of steam;
Resting beside the Levers of Control
That only He must touch.

"Righto, mate!": the tender's full;
And as the fireman stows the crane
The Post Office whistlers and the train guard
Secure the mail cage
And thunderslam the loading doors ("Poor pussycats!").
Dad's kissed and dismissed: he's away to London for the day.
At the train's first door he climbs aboard,
Lowers the window, and leans out to listen
To Sir Edward's refrain.

Bells ting in the box;
Down swings the signal arm.

Here comes the Station Master in his Hat,
And blacked-to-brillance Sergeant Major shoes,
To see this train
– The Cathedrals Express, the most important of the morning –
On its Great Western way.

Back in the cab now, the nimble fireman
Toils flame-faced,
Quick-feeding the coal with ringing clangs.
We see the chimney-haze turn grey:
Aeon-ancient trees become propulsive potential.

The last door's slammed; a way away the green flag's held aloft.
The Station Master nods,
And leaning from his special door
(Marked GUARD)
The Guard acknowledges the far flag with his own.

He shrills his Acme Thunderer;
And over
Shovel-scrape on bunker plates,
Blower roar and ejector-chortle,
Heating pipe hisses, and
The thirsty injectors' gargoyle guzzling
He bellows to the driver
"RIGHT AWAY!"

"Mind your ears!",
The thoughtful driver calls.
He reaches near the roof to work the whistle:
Sir Edward calls the city to Attention.

And even
Heaven
Holds its breath
To listen.

WHEREVER WE GO

Wherever we go, whenever we go, however we go:
A Sunday ride, a night-time swim,
A blue-skied walk through snow…
Whatever we do outside, we know
That we are so
Lucky.

Lucky in an old boat, shabby but proud;
Lucky in hand-me-down clothes, faded now.
Lucky, using rubber bands to tidy our hair;
Lucky, though our bicycles often need repairs.
Lucky, lucky, lucky, because – WE WERE THERE!

We have sailed a long while with dolphins playing round about;
We've discovered orchards lost for years:
Oh, such delicious fruit!
We've swum down deep through crystal waters,
Glimpsing Neptune's mystic realm;
Roaming cliff forts of our ancestors,
We've travelled back through time.

It's a wonderful invention, The Great Outdoors,
Because Nature doesn't care if you are rich or you are poor.
You can sail on a raft, don't need anything to swim;
Just look after yourselves, and those great big grins
Will show the whole world that you did the right thing:
With the blessing and encouragement of Mum and Dad,
You came, you saw, you DID!

So – wherever you go, whoever you are,
Whether you're living close or afar,
We hope, how we hope, that *your* countryside
Isn't just something you see from inside
A stuffy,
Boring,
Safety-locked car.

You must tell them, your parents, and make it very plain:
'Yes, I really do need to go out in the rain!
I want to go exploring where I might get muddy,
And I know that if I tumble, then my knees could get bloody.
Oh, so what if I last came back with burrs in my hair,
And a rip in my shirt from *here* to *there*?
There's a whole flipping Universe, just beyond that door:
Better let me explore it, or it WON'T BE FAIR!'

Let them go, Mum; let them, Dad:
Of course you will worry, but you'll be so glad
When you see them come home, filthy and tired
But, under all that dirt, so inspired.
Wherever they go, your children will
Remember their adventures for so very long…
Until, one day, there'll be someone looking up, pleading:
'*Do* let us stay out for another hour, this evening!'

OLD RUSSIAN FREIGHTER

Dedicated to unhappy sailors of any nationality. Modern merchant ships may be more comfortable, but would you like being anchored in St Brides Bay, enduring day after day of winter gales…?

Up and down enormous swells on the Atlantic Ocean,
Our captain's full of vodka and we've got a crazy bosun.
Our ship is really ancient and we spend each day in fear;
And all our lives depend upon a one-eyed engineer.
Not one of us is on this ship because we volunteered –
But we all know much better than to argue with superiors.

German sailors: very lucky, lots of apple strudel.
Chinese ships don't serve you chips – but lots of filling noodles.
Korean cooks have recipe books for Pekinese and poodles,
But what can Russians ever buy with hardly any roubles?
Our guts are rumbling all the time, our farts are truly savage –
But what can you expect when all we get to eat is cabbage?

Join the navy, see the world: that's what they always tell you –
But in the Soviet merchant fleet, sightseeing is off the menu.
When we got to London town we tied up to an oiler,
And all our time in Singapore, we worked inside the boiler.
From time to time the Captain says~
'I'm giving you some shore leave,' –
But that is when we go to Hull, and never at the Maldives.

We're supposed to be so proud we keep the red flag flying –
And say that we will fight for Russia, happy to be dying.
We're supposed to love Joe Stalin, but it's very trying
To tell you that we're happy when you know that we are lying.
Perhaps one day there'll come the chance~
Of free and fair elections…
But till it comes just grit your teeth~
And cope with the dejection.

Musical score: Page 136

Wouldn't it be wonderful to have a cosy fo'c'sle?
Wouldn't it be lovely to end the watch with cocoa?
How I'd love to eat a meal with meat and lots of gravy,
What I'd give to jump ship and join any other navy.
Let's tramp about the Coral Sea instead of round the Arctic–
Comrade, count your blessings: we have never been to Cardiff!

THE OTHER MISTER BLACK

You might have heard me tell the tale of a cat called Mister Black;
His hunting ground was Trehill, way down the Deer Park track.
Well, you'd better know there's another cat,
Goes by the selfsame name –
But this Mister Black has earned himself
A different sort of fame.

It's easier to find him, 'cos he's not inclined to hide:
Just mosey down to his house, and the garden gate beside
Will lead you past his Bantam Cocks and his Rhode Island Reds...
'Til there, beyond the apple tree, you'll find a wooden shed.
And if you peer inside it, you'll see instruments galore,
Plus amplifiers, and speakers, and microphones, and more:
For in this secret hideaway in furthest Pembrokeshire
Is a sixteen-track recording rig – and sometimes, it's for hire!

There's a powerful computer, and a wall-full of CDs:
Country, Western, Rolling Stones, JJ Cale's *Call me the Breeze;*
For this cat, he lives for music, both the listening and playing:
His heartbeat's like a bass drum, that's what sassy folks are saying.
So if someone needs a song laid down, or overdubs, or more,
They tread that bumpy backyard path to Mister Black's shed door
– Except, this name is not the one that those musicians use:
When they raise a glass to praise him, it's...

"ALL HAIL, **MISTER BLUES**!"

A HARD FROST ON THE COAST

The surf sounds so brightly
On this freezing night.
How far inshore, still clear,
Each wave-fall can be heard!

All else seems still,
Save the silent sky-arc
Of Strumble's light,
And, across the bay, trembling glimmers.

The frost has stopped the stream;
So, whilst foxes hunt, cats prowl,
And owls patrol,
It is only the sea we hear moving
Under the brittle stars.

STANDING OUT TO SEA

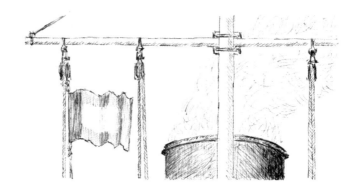

You had, for a long while,
Been flying the Blue Peter –
Announcing,
READY TO DEPART.

Now the gangplank has been hauled aboard
And stowed
And the telegraph, already set to STAND BY,
Rings once more,
Its pointer moving to SLOW AHEAD.

The last hawser is cast off;
And, as the wakening engine stirs the harbour's waters,
Between your no-longer-weary hull
And the familiar quay
A gap begins to open.

You may look old-fashioned,
But you still look *right*,
As you always did:
That was the way of your generation.
You stand out to sea now, as ever,
Proud and determined.

The evening's low sun suits you, lights you well;
As you turn for the West,
So glad we are
That you will be following the Sun,
Preventing it from setting:
Departing with it,
You will at last
Be there to see what new land it will rise over
In that imminent morning, mysterious,
Out there beyond our horizon.

Your berth here will remain empty,
For no other craft
Could ever take that place;
So we, who have to stay,
Must rely for comfort
On our many memories –
And, of course, upon each other.

There!
We see it, every one of us
Who waves from the sea wall:
That which we had so hoped for –
A last glint from your brightwork
Which signals,
Like a knowing wink…
ALL WILL BE WELL.

FLAMELAND

It has been such a long power cut that
The candle's now just a low stump,
Beginning to burn blue and smell more of wick than wax;
But they, sister and brother, don't care,
There before the fire.

Side by pyjama'd side they sprawl the rug;
And, chins propped by cupped hands,
Elbows nudging Granny's gleaming fender,
On they stare into that story-full smallhuge world:
Their imaginations are playing in Flameland.

Flameland:
Like a binoculared orange sunset made oh-so complicated
By tangled clouds whose purple shades
Are shot with lemony rays...
The harder you concentrate,
The more you see.

The embers of a plank offcut become
A range of red-hot hills,
Pinnacled with white-cracked charcoal castles;
That gas-flaring volcano was once
Some stubborn oak-knot
Their father's oathing axe thrice baulked at.

Minute metal flakes from some special sort of sea-paint,
Momentarily incandescent as searing oxygen consumes –
They become here-and-gone sparkling white fairies...
Or, for him, searchlight-betrayed bombers,
Thousand-Fahrenheit blooming
As the incendiaries and fuel in their bellies rippingly ignite,
Three miles above that firestorm fellow raiders created.

As for her turquoise and ultramarine fire-djinns…
Their glass-transparent mesmerising dances
Mark the melting-places, she knows,
Of fixings which once clenched planks together,
Always watertight,
For a boat-crafter with a well-earned reputation,
Long since departed his building-yard.

Now vaporised, those metal molecules
(Mostly copper, zinc, tin, and phosphorus –
but also cobalt, judging from those colours)
Fly up from the flame-tips
And, riding out from the chimney mouth far above,
Their fading heat
Momentarily
Shimmers the light of the very star-furnaces
Such as once created those heavier chemical elements,
Long before our Mother Earth was ever conceived.

TERNS

Making every wind-twist advantageous,
They scoop along the shore
Confidently, although with seeming risk
So close to the breakers' lips
That their wings must be surely wetted
By the horsemane mists furling there
Like aircraft wake vortices.

Those fine beaks have subtlety;
They aren't for stabbing, dragging, and gagging down:
Unlike gulls, terns don't rip rubbish from bags,
Or steal from human hands.
Lighter than the sea-thieves, more flexibly-framed,
Their flight is especially graceful in its darting,
Which today starks white against those shinglegrey sleet squalls
Threatening drenchdown upon our holms.

They've skimmed this beach edge for short minutes…
And that's enough!
Now they're off out to sea again,
Seeking we know not what away south-west.
They'll skydance round that storm, perhaps;
Or go directly horizonwards to only know the ocean –
And live landlessly unworried for many imagined days.

THE STREAM AND I

Here are the stream and I, together hurrying down
This humble outcrop-weaving valley,
Under a sky of chill blue.

Why the rush, this calm grass-flavoured morning,
Past clumpy banks dew-lushed to silveriness
And chiffchaffing thickets…?
Because, look: there beyond the fork in the road
Which the fast fresh water ducks under, momentarily culverted,
The sea has come to meet us both.

This, the almanac predicted, should be the year's highest tide:
The Gann saltings are fully submerged,
And the still-rising mirror-surfaced flood
Has burst through bank gaps
To inundate already brackish pastures.

However, although the old bridge arch I now stand above
Must hold its breath,
The keystone having succumbed to that up-inching meniscus,
Those bubbling pools which encroach upon
The long-carless tarmac from either side,
Approaching each other to very nearly…
Actually, they never get to kiss.

For the Earth's turning has already brought us to –
Slack Water.

Slack Water:
The brimmed reach's weedclumped swan-distanced smoothness
Reflecting a white gold Sun;
Reflecting, too, the moos of confused cows,
Watching from their sea-hedged meadow…

…Who have in fact noticed, well before us,
Garish human movement, heading Northwards
From Dale's sleepy bay:
Two double kayaks, soon to be bow-bumping
The parapet we perch on, keeping feet dry.

They cheese for a silly photo
Before awaying, keels wiggling, strong paddle-strokes slurpy,
Back downriver, course set for the bacon sarnies
Which await them in a Peugeot boot at Pickleridge.

Slack Water:
The level will rise no further –
As it surely would have done with lower air pressure,
Or had a strong sou'wester been heaping seas
Into the Haven's mouth.

So, very soon, the sea starts retreating;
And I and the other watchers prepare to depart,
Glad to have been there and seen –
But all, like superlative-loving children,
Disappointed.

For we know that tides in previous years,
On paper less impresssive,
Have caused much more inundation,
Well-swamping history's old crossing
And even completely covering
The new bridge's approach road.

But then…
Isn't that Nature's prerogative,
To always keep us guessing?
To keep us marking "HT 7.7M+"
On the kitchen calendars of future years?

GOLD IN THE BANK!

Gold in the bank, gold in the bank:
Again, dear friends, I have gold in the bank!
Gold in the bank, gold in the bank...
And it's wonderful Nature that I must thank.

Oh, I don't mean the metal that causes so much trouble,
And I don't mean the bank on the High Street, there in town:
I'm talking about my daffodils, all bursting out this morning
In the bank which faces southwards, shining emerald in the sun.

After Autumn's copper leaves
Which followed August's bronze-brown children,
We had December's iron furrows and its lead and pewter seas;
Then came February's silver frosts,
With her mercury-bright icicles
And that platinum patina: furry hoar frost in the trees.

But now the climbing sun, it teeters on the Equinox's seesaw;
Thus, today, it's WARMTH that greets us
As we venture out of doors;
And without the toil of miners, or of crushers, or refiners –
As sly Zeus came to coy Danäe, see that shimmering bounty pour!

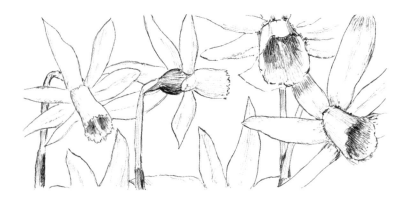

CHECKING THE CHAINS

On two successive middays, usually about the middle of March –
That's when it happens.
It starts with cars congregating along the ridge road,
Regardless of the weather.

If it is calm and fine,
Drivers will stand around staring seawards,
Chatting boatily.
If the wind's bitter, they'll hunch in their vehicles,
Slurping flask-slopped soup and crunching oaty crackers,
With Radio Four on, but nervously unheard until it's time for
'AND NOW, ATTENTION ALL SHIPPING...'

On wet days, each man will now and then
Wind down tea-steamed windows
To binocular through the precipitation,
And inspect the sea/shore interface.
Then, consulting maritime almanacs,
And estimating the influence of today's wind,
(Considering what the Den's barometer said before they left),
They will try to adjust for the conditions.

There is much clock-checking today because it approaches:
A phenomenon foreseeable even by our mariner ancestors –
Such is the formality of the planets' dances around each other,
And with their mother star.

In the backs of hatches and estate cars,
New-chain-laden wheelbarrows are brightly heavy.
There, too, in strong buckets, Castrol pots gleam,
And pliers and grips and wrenches chromely shine;
Meanwhile, inanimately impatient,
Shackles wait in well-greased silence...

There's a stirring: the moment has come.

Kit is grabbed and, hats and gloves tugged on,
People are suddenly hurrying.
They top the ridge, equipped,
Like Tommies quitting their trenches –
Only these today confront just the East wind,
Not Flanders air insane with lead.
No: nothing will stop this splattering amateur charge
To the emerging sinkers,
And the only enemies out there on the flats today
Are time, mud, cold, and corrosion.

Such an ecstasy of cold-fingered fumbling: oh, the obstinacy of
Weed-stinking barnacled buoys, unobliging sea-eroded shackles,
Seized swivels that absorb such quantities of curses,
And slippery, self-kinking, knuckle-nicking wire!
The blue hands, bloody with scratches;
The swear words when catching sight of
Apparently turbocharged watch-hands:
Still there are jobs left but already the barrow,
So much lightened, seems tempted to
Go bobbing off up the River Gann
As the tide surgingly returns…!

It is Mooring Maintenance Day.

OPENING NIGHT

For the younger members of DADS – Dale Amateur Dramatic Society

When young feet first stand on this stage,
How fast young hearts are beating!
How tight the ribs, how tense all nerves,
While cheeks and brows start heating.
That wait, before it's time to speak
Or, even braver, sing –
How long it seems, while lights blaze down
And many eyes are staring.

Young blood forced fast, young breaths so quick;
Young brains, which want to race;
Yet they know that they mustn't:
Acting wants a steady pace.
We must all rein in our bodies,
We who strive to tell a story;
We thus will please our audience,
And so succeed, with glory!

WE WENT OUTSIDE

Ten o'clock on a March evening: Dale Amateur Dramatic Society has just presented the first night of its show, based on **The Sound of Music**, *and it has been rapturously received.*

The junior singers, superbly trained by our resident opera star, have changed out of their costumes and now await their lifts home…

In case you're wondering, the "somebody" is me.

We went outside to play in the dark
That Thursday, after the show;
Just to let off steam, and have a lark –
So excited, after the show!

But there was something special about that night,
We saw it, straight away:
Not a breath of wind stirred anywhere
Out there in Dale Bay.

The trees were still, and even the clouds
Hung motionless, lit by the moon;
The air was warm, so warm you'd believe
That the month wasn't March, but June.

And the sea was flat like a summer lake,
No waves splashed on the shore;
It reflected the Haven's distant lights–
A dark mirror, stretching far.

We had none of us ever known it so calm
As it was that magic evening,
Which made somebody say to us, walking past,
'I really think you should sing.'

We rushed to the end of the old sea wall,
And stood side by side, hand-in-hand,
And we all agreed we should try "Goodbye!",
So that was what we sang.

'Goodbye!', we sang, and again 'Goodbye!',
And every time sang louder;
And the echoes they came back from the woods
And from the cliffs, and further.

With every call we felt our voices
Clearer, surer, stronger...
And back they rang from across the water,
Resounding ever longer.

Might there never be a night as calm
Again in my life, I wonder?
It seems that Nature means to send us
Ever more gales and thunder.

So I won't forget that wonderful time
When we sang to the sea and the sky,
And back from the gloom our voices came –
'Goodbye!, Goodbye!, Goodbye...!'
'Goodbye!'

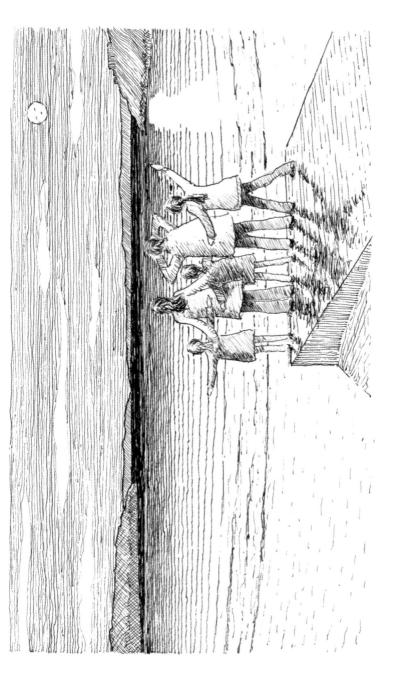

RUNWAYSKILN FARM, 6TH APRIL

Blackthorn's blossom-time beginning:
Broached buds whitely blaze,
Stark as bleached cotton
Against this hasty blue sky.

A blackbird we've startled bolts into the blackthorn bush,
There to compose himself, a breeze-bounced stem thin-gripped;
And, that spike-defended shelter emboldening him,
His song now blooms.

ONE'S HAD ENOUGH!

Inspired by the 2012 Diamond Jubilee celebrations; dedicated to those many unnoticed heroes who make up the Royal entourage, and quietly and efficiently make sure that every official engagement is completely successful, down to the last detail.

One has a rather special job: there's lots of travelling round
For, all across the British Isles, one has to visit towns.
Now, some of these are ugly, and some of them are quaint—
But when will people realise that one hates the smell of paint?

It's true, there's never litter: the streets are spick and span;
And every police officer is smiling, to a man.
One never, ever, ever, gets jostled by the crowd
As they wave their flags and cheer: ~
My goodness, aren't they loud?

One week one is in Scotland; the next, one is in Wales;
But they never let one stop to shop: one misses all the sales!
It's best behaviour every time: one must never lose one's cool—
Even with some dense official who's being such a fool.

The work, it hasn't altered at all in sixty years—
They couldn't mechanise it; that never was one's fear.
But, all around, the world has changed; ~
A huge difference, of course, is,
When one started there were debutantes, ~
And every girl loved horses.

So don't you think one's justified at least to mull it over
When, at one's time of life, it's off we go again to Dover,
Or Penzance, bound for Tresco, or darkest Pembrokeshire?
So many thousand miles! Oh, why not jolly well retire?

Of course one was delighted when first one got the job;
And one can't deny that, down the years, ~
One's earned a fair few bob.
But now, at last, the day has come: ~
This work, one's going to chuck it:
Someone else can follow Liz's coach with a shovel and a bucket!

SPRING

Wedged into a snug sunny corner
Between two big hay bales, up in my paddock,
I am out of the south-east wind.
Here I pen-muse,
Perched on a beer crate –
For this lush grass, which looks so sprawlable,
Was rain-lashed all last night.

Nature and man make Spring a noisy event:
Gulls bicker and gutsache more than ever;
Tractors, guzzling fuel,
Plough, fertilise, and lime;
Lambs and their mums bleat back and forth
Across the Marloes Court fields.

The new house, going up behind the old Post Office,
Is still no more than a timber skeleton awaiting its brick skin –
And as such it makes a superb soundbox, which reverberates
Tribally to the tom-tom beat of Kevan the carpenter's hammer...

And it sends forth an amplified roar
Across the whole village,
Grating into wincing ears,
When his power plane swiftly eats the millimetres
Off pale-as-paper new-sawn pine.

The world smells of Spring that strongly now,
Everything which is outdoors
– Including the cold north yard,
Which you'd think quite dead –
Has its own awakening scent;
So, I suppose, even concrete-loving lichens
Must be up to something.

Primroses, grasses, and especially sliced soil:
All fulminate with a newnessness,
Which carries sharply green
And darkly fecund
On the moisture-sweetened air.

Returning from tidal foraging on the Gann,
Restless-sounding geese overfly the house.
They will surely all have gone soon…

But, I wonder,
Will the swallows be back in my shed,
And measuring up for urgent nests,
Before Easter Sunday?

Easter Sunday –
When St Peter's bell
Will clang hard and long
For celebration
Of a Christian date,
Of these fast-lengthening days,
And the pagan bursting of buds.

BLUEBELLS

Bluebells dancing in the breeze,
Bluebells dancing by the sea:
Such a sight to please the eye,
So much blue beneath the sky!
Bluebells make the air so sweet,
In the wild, or in the street.
It's the perfume we love best:
Scent of bluebells from the West.

Bluebells growing round the church,
Bluebells all about the porch:
Dancing bluebells – hear them ring,
Calling folk to pray and sing.
Bluebell islands in the West,
Bluer than the ocean's crest:
All the sailors from their ships
See bluebells dancing on the cliffs.

Bluebells in the woodland glade,
Where young hearts declare their love;
Will it last, and will they wed…?
Time it takes, true love to prove.
Bluebells, bluebells, truest blue –
I don't ask for gems from you;
I won't want a sapphire ring
As long as bluebells bloom in spring.

Bluebells in the month of May,
Dancing all the warm long day,
When the puffins have returned,
And swallows fly around our homes.
After winter, cold and glum,
Bluebells tell us Spring has come;
Summer makes them disappear…
But they will be back next year!

Musical score: Page 140

BLUES MAN

Inspired by Andy Rowlands, a truly accomplished musician.

He sometimes plays a solo cigarette;
He likes to sing his roll-your-own guitar.
He drives his own electric songs;
He smokes an old red car.

COAST-BORN

Slender, fine, and light, she;
Her skin wears the sun with joy.
Her walk's the happiest dance and,
Running with laughter in the salty wind,
This horizon-eyed gymnast seems airborne…
Who came into the world sea-sweet:
How ever sure, her swimming –
How always easy, diving deep!

When she looks up
From a depth of outdoor thought,
The smile which greets the tall green world
Is enough to seize Nature's breath.
So heartfully loving to those she knows
This truest of friends is – and always will be:
No fire, no storm, nor even flood,
Shall ever defeat that spirit!

PORT LION

Bird-silvered to echoing, the tideline-overreaching woods
Which hill this inlet with westerly shelter;
Stream creased and crumble-edged,
Those morning-sheened mud banks
Whose bee-busy stubbly margins
Footprint many a land bird's curiosity.

Sleekly silhouetted
Against the broad river's petty scintillation,
Slumbering yachts (a few not nicely opulent)
Weathervane today's northerly breeze,
While a southbound ebb compounds every mooring's tension.

A flappy jay bisects my view:
Jaggedly loud, a colourful knife
Ripping across my sketched peace –
It and those magpies pursuant, disputing devil-birds.

Following the three heated flights I notice,
Far beyond,
Where ripples lap a coalgritty sandbank,
Two busy swan necks.
Surprisingly white-dark against the sun,
With squinting difficulty I study them…
They are not dredging, but preening.

A short walk, now, to unfold my map's up-river view –
And I am astonished
By that Presceli peak's apparent closeness
In the Scottish clarity
Of this cool Irish wind.

After long contemplating a clinker hulk
Wearied to sinking by years of unlove…

For so many generations, this now Nature-loud arena
Surely resounded to
The bash and rasp of boatbuilding,
The rumble and clatter of carts and cargoes;
Heard, too, at the top of each once-upon-a-tide,
The shouts, scaly slaps, and willowy creaks
Of live fish, being sold straight off the bottomboards
Of pitchblack villagers' dinghies
And slithered into grass nested home-woven baskets.

But now, here's just an Ordnance co-ordinate
Whose only memories
Which mud hasn't buried or rot consumed
Are officially absent, condemned by sterile "heritage"
To gather obscurity's dust
Somewhere under the County Library.

47

DON'T BE AFRAID!

To the tune of *Lord of the Dance*

1

There once was a nurse who carried a lamp,
Treating wounded soldiers in a camp;
The generals said that her efforts would fail –
But she was Florence Nightingale.

CHORUS

When in your heart you know that you are right,
Defend yourself, but never start a fight;
Don't be afraid of the storm or the night,
And always turn your face to the light!

2

There once was a man, and he had a dream:
A great iron ship which was driven by steam.
Everybody said, "You can't build that!" –
But this was the man with a tall black hat.
(Chorus)

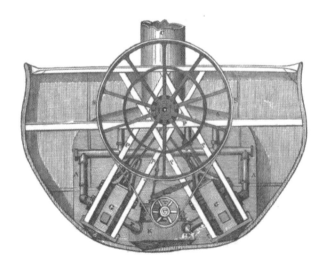

3
There once was a Dutch boy who went for a hike;
He saw that the sea was breaking through a dyke!
He stopped that water 'til help could arrive,
And alone he saved many thousand lives.
(Chorus)

4
A girl called Anne had to hide in a house;
She wrote down her story, quiet as a mouse.
She never knew that one day it would be
The most famous diary in history.
(Chorus)

5
There once was man, and he gave a speech:
"We shall fight them on the hills, ~
We shall fight them on the beach!"
All that he promised us was blood, sweat, and tears –
We won that war after six long years.
(Chorus)

VIKING RAIDERS

Viking raiders, Viking raiders –
Or, this time, are they invaders?
Viking raiders, Viking raiders,
Slicing through the waves!

Viking killers from the North lands,
Bloody faces, bloody sword-hands,
Bloody beaches where their ships land:
Death rides on the waves!

Viking terror, crushing Shetland,
Sweeping through the English wetlands:
Put to death the Saxon yeoman
As his family cries!

Viking sailors, quickly learning,
Ever westward is their yearning:
Down the Irish Sea go burning,
Celtic gold's the prize!

Viking oar-strokes, quick and even;
Viking eyes, as sharp as ravens':
Finding now a mighty Haven
In the west of Wales.

Viking bows cut sheltered waters,
Viking swords sing as they slaughter;
Save the wives and spare the daughters:
Need them for their slaves!

Viking settlers, swords grown colder,
Less blood spilt as they get older;
Farmers' worries weight their shoulders–
Fathers' worries, too!

Viking raiders: now, they're history,
And your family's past's a mystery;
But your fair hair tells a story:
You're a Viking true…!

Musical score: Page 141

I'M A CRONK

I'm a CRONK!, I'm a CRONK!, I'm a raven:
A very big, very black bird.
My demeanour is dramatic,
And I'm good at aerobatics;
But, yes, I must admit, my song is not the best you've heard.
I'm a CRONK!, I'm a CRONK!, I'm a raven.
I'm a CRONK!, I'm a CRONK!, I'm a raven.

I'm a CRONK!, I'm a CRONK!, I'm a raven,
With very sharp, very wise eyes.
They-ey are so bright and knowing,
That's intelligence they're showing:
As a thinker I am equal to you – that's what I surmise.
I'm a CRONK!, I'm a CRONK!, I'm a raven.
I'm a CRONK!, I'm a CRONK!, I'm a raven.

I'm a CRONK!, I'm a CRONK!, I'm a raven:
The Bird Of Fate, always, in books.
So you know, when I appear,
Good friend Death is drawing near –
Especially when someone gets a very nasty look!
I'm a CRONK!, I'm a CRONK!, I'm a raven.
I'm a CRONK!, I'm a CRONK!, I'm a raven.

I'm a CRONK!, I'm a CRONK!, I'm a raven,
Merlin once kept me in his tower:
If I wanted to I could tell
You about his very good spells;
But, trusting Man with magic? – Never in a million years!
I'm a CRONK!, I'm a CRONK!, I'm a raven.
I'm a CRONK!, I'm a CRONK!, I'm a raven.

I'm a CRONK!, I'm a CRONK!, I'm a raven:
A century's nothing to me!
I've seen Cleopatra's warships and
The Vikings in their Norse ships…
And I'll still be here when there's no-one left to sail the seas!
I'm a CRONK!, I'm a CRONK!, I'm a raven.
I'm a CRONK!, I'm a very old raven;
I'm a CRONK!, I can see into heaven;
I'm a CRONK!, Read the soul of a bad man;
I'm a CRONK!, And I know all about you!
I'm a CRONK!, I'm a CRONK!, I'm a CRONK!
CRONK!, CRONK!, CRONK!

CRONK!

CRONK!

CRONK!

Musical score: Page 142

SOUND ADVICE

Leaving behind anything unnecessary
– Meaning everything modern –
Take yourself to an empty shore.
Go alone, or with one good and quiet-loving friend.

Some sunny shelter found, settle yourself
And listen only to the waves:
Their reliable crunching roar
Will wash all worries away, then make you sleep…

When you wake,
There and then will be the place and time
– Accompanied or not –
For you to thoughtfully talk.

THE BUMB OF THE FLIGHTLEBEE

The bumb of the flightlebee,
Hummle its genting,
Gardinds every remener
That Comer is summing.

The birdness of sweetsong
From trees in the up
Chilspires all the indren
To glee round with dance.

The wild of the scentflowers
Laning the edge:
How perperb their sufume,
In rainshine or sun!

All the greens flash bright leave
As the sing gently breezes:
So much gar, in our joydens,
In Springain, in Brit!

JUNE DUSK

We could, we all agree, easily read a book by this late, late light;
Strongest, in it, is the colour of foxgloves still unfolding.

Our seaward progress panics a rabbit:
Away it hurtles, as if propelled by a tripped spring…
As, suddenly, do several others!
Foolishly scattering from where they had been crouching
– Unseen, quite safe –
These young ones haven't yet learned tactics:
Luckily for them,
We have neither dog nor gun.

Unsurprisingly, buzzards now show much interest in grasslands.

Though the swell-filled shore roars like a great weir,
The air's humidity bears no sticky riveriness:
Salt and clean is the breeze which the steep cliff lifts off the sea
For flower-tall meadows and honeysuckled hedges to sweeten.

A badger, hungry because of last night's rain,
Blunders from cover noisily;
Upwind, not scenting us,
It diagonals the coast path close ahead.

This ten o'clock sheep-bleated dimness,
This almost-longest of evenings,
Is dustily fluttered by moths stirring from verge grasses.
Thus bats trench Castle Rag lane again, and again –
Sometimes turning before us,
Sometimes pattering on past, close overhead.
Their hunting flight: more jinked
Than that of the slipperiest fighter pilot –
Who ever kept his wings intact.

There's the first star, at last!
It signals that the Battle of Bedtime has been lost.

And so, conceding defeat,
The children shout curt farewells to each horizon ship,
Then quickly quit the Beacon.
We call after their homeward,
Their shower-bound scamperdown,
'You're to share one apple tonight!'
Because, they having so stretched the surfy afternoon,
Supper wasn't that long ago.

ESTUARY

This breeze!
So busily it travels,
Seemingly stirring not just the trees...
For, surely, along each mooringed pill
It whispers into frustrated rigging.

We hope they aren't hollow, the air's promises of weekend sails;
For all of these yachts must itch
To un-mud their keels,
Escape the hated restraint of buoy-strops and,
Standing out to the True Sea, shake off this brackish lethargy.

The wind now lures our eyes: observing its trajectory,
They notice the mariners' entice, there far away;
For, ultimately,
Beyond where the widespread flow sweeps east,
Light's silver mirth can just be seen
To double back westwards –
Atlantic-bound!

Reining ourselves away from Water's eternal attraction,
We look around this calm-floored pill head –
And, peering into its jungly greenery, realise:
This roadway was, long ago since,
Pickaxe-hacked out of the redstone bank.
Thus, we stand upon
Not some naturally-useful streamside bluff,
But a purposed quay.

And so,
As we have found so frequently elsewhere,
When we stop and listen to the tale
This sea-valley's landscape can silently tell,
Here too was once enslaved.

Enslaved to those very darknesses of darknesses: the
Boy-stooping, man-crushing, sometimes all-drowning
Coal measures.

We sense them down there, fathoms beneath us:
Eternally staggering pain-wracked,
Writhing back and forth and up and down and side to side,
Evermore contorted by faulting's crushing inquisition,
While everywhere pent with ambush-poised water…

Here, the old days were not good
If you had to fodder a mine.

THE END OF THE VOYAGE

Dale is sometimes visited by historic craft which offer adventurous holidays to people who aren't content with lazing on the beach, and want to get a feel for life under sail – albeit with rather better comfort and cuisine than crews enjoyed in the old days!

It was the arrival one quiet evening of a preserved pilot cutter which inspired this admittedly sentimental song.

Now here we are, back in our home port safe and well;
The anchor's down, and we have furled all of the sails.
The sun is setting, and the sky turns darkest blue;
There is no watch to keep for captain or for crew.
We have sailed far, in waters wide and wild,
Seen vessels lost, to death been reconciled;
Hot were the tropics, and so strange the Northern Lights:
Such memories: we have enough to last a life.

Now thanks I give to every member of the crew:
We worked as one: it was as one that we came through.
There was a time, each one did save another's life:
Thus all will soon return to home and hearth and love.
And praise we send to those who built our ship:
She never flinched, nor tired as we did;
Whate'er the wind, she always answered to the wheel;
Whate'er the waves, she always kept a steadfast keel.

What next will pass? – 'Tis only Fate can truly know;
But we must face the cloudy future full of hope.
Change there will be in all our lives, we can be sure;
But we all trust our shipboard friendships will endure.
And so we light our lamps as it grows dark
And as the stars start burning like bright sparks,
Let's all hold hands, and we shall dance the night away;
When morning comes – there will begin another day!

Musical score: Page 146

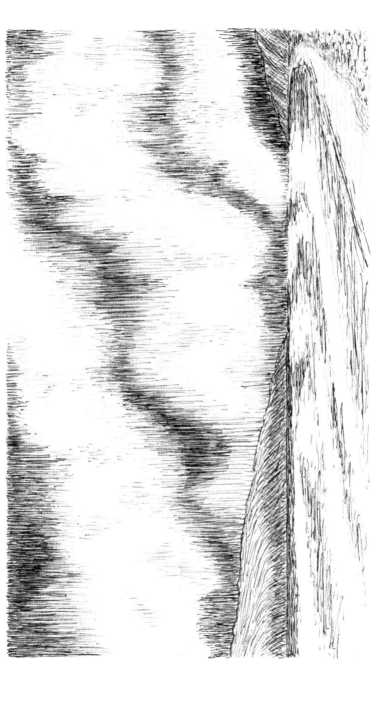

TOO HOT FOR AN OTTER

When the weather's getting hotter
It is no fun for an otter, 'cos he's really got a lot, a lot of fur.
He will give his paws a *Click*!
And say, 'Gosh, I need a dip!'
And he'll slip down 'til he's right beside the water.

And as soon as he is in,
Then the cooling will begin–
And our otter friend will say 'Now that's much better!'
Getting wetter, he feels fitter;
Then he has a little titter:
'If I'd got much hotter, I'd have turned into an otter fritter!'

Otter doesn't whizz and splash,
'Cos his tum is full of fish,
And he's practised every sort of dive and swim;
So on his back he floats, and pretends that he's a boat:
He has no need of exercise, not him.

Horrid sun, for being a rotter
And for overheating otters:
It is really too, too much for them to bear!
They've no sunscreen; they've no hats;
And they don't like heat like cats;
And their thick fur coats are worse
Than wearing thermal underwear!

Now he will stay there in the water
As all good otters really ought to
When it's as hot here
As it is in Timbuktu,
So he stretches himself out
And then sinks down
'Til just his snout
Is the only part which isn't out of view.

Let us go now,
Let us leave:
He can snooze there in the reeds,
Biding time until the sun dips to the sea;
But once it has got dark,
The little fishes must look sharp—
Or they'll end up being Mister Otter's tea!

OF COURSE!

Of course I NEED another snorkel: the water is so clear,
And it really is quite warm, and this little cove's so dear –
And the super-special treat for us is…
No-one else is here!

I've learned to swim round very quietly, without a single splash,
So the fish aren't bothered by me: they never make a dash
To hide beneath a rock, or skulk in seaweed dense and green –
Even when, with special effort, I dive a long way down.
I can skim the shining sand below, a sea-nymph tanned so brown,
While silver creatures play above, all shimmery in the sun!
So this isn't just an afternoon of underwater fun…
It's my best adventure ever – ever since my life began!
Because there aren't just fishes to be looked at down below:
There are many other animals, whose names I do not know;
Plus hermit crabs, and shore crabs, big spider crabs as well –
I admit, those used to scare me when I was a younger girl.

…Of course I have persuaded my parents to agree:
I fill my lungs and, turning round, I slip beneath the sea.
I say a prayer to thank them as I frog-kick down once more:
Other children miss so much, just swimming near the shore!

OVER THE TOP

Such a graceless girl,
That pasty girl:
Such a huffy,
Such a hasty girl!

So cool, she thought, it had to be
To wear high heels down to the sea:
Sensible, grippy, sturdy sandals
Meant a fashion disaster she couldn't handle!

Under too-floppy hat,
A stroppy scowl;
And make-up, laid on
With a trowel.

With tasteless tee
And skin-tight shorts,
All sloppy speech
And empty thoughts…

While on the 'phone to her mate Garth,
As she tottered down the Coastal Path,
So busy with 'Do WHAT–? As if!'…
She stumbled, and fell off the cliff.

SHIPS

Saint George's Channel — sometimes unofficially called The Celtic Sea — lies between West Wales and South East Ireland. As you'd expect, much local sea traffic crosses and re-crosses; that aside, being the outlet from the Irish Sea into the Western Approaches of the Atlantic Ocean, this stretch of water is a very busy international shipping route, used by many large craft voyaging to and from the deepwater ports and oil and gas terminals of the North Sea, or the Baltic states, or even Russian territory beyond The North Cape.

That Channel is so busy, there are rules for navigating it: out beyond the remote Smalls rocks with their lonely lighthouse, vessels steam along well-separated Northbound and Southbound shipping lanes rather like vehicles rolling on a motorway; however, because they are so far from land, even the slightest haze in the air means that their progress is not visible from our shores. We locals go about our business not seeing them, and only subconscious of their presence; but many visitors have no idea how heavily used those waters are — and are therefore astounded when the clear air of crisp cold nights reveals many clusters of lights sliding silently along the horizon...

Those countless ships: even if you never notice them, it doesn't mean they aren't out there!

This poem works really well read by four voices, taking lines in turn — except for the words I have underlined, which everyone should deliver together, with gusto!

Bulkers, tankers, tugs with lighters,
Small ships, big ships, sheep-and-pig ships,
Black ships, grey ships, white ships, lightships,
Banana ships in undercoat,
Ships you wouldn't think would float,
(Yawn!) There goes the Rosslare boat.

In-by-day-and-out-by-night ships,
Gas ships: orange 'cos they might go…
BANG!

Steel ships, Kiel ships, down-at-heel ships,
Ships on a quick trip, home by tea.

Ship ships, car ships, rubbish-for-the-tip ships
Freezer ships, reefer ships,
Ships which can break ice,
Ships which can make ice,
Ships bringing tonic, lemons, and gin,
Trying to keep up with our Gran.

Octane,
Floating cranes (all eyes on the weather vane),
Irish ferry – yet again!
Clank-clank-clanking ships
Pulling up the anchor chain,
Ships from the Spanish Main,
Ships for the Isle of Grain,
Half-laden, light in ballast, or deep.

Potatoes-going-for-chips ships,
Parsnip ships and turnip ships,
Greens ships with cabbages
<u>And tons of farty sprouts.</u>
Battleships, cattleships
Ships that go hoot, **HOOT**!
Ones that carry fruit;
Ones that carry loot.

Russky oil pipe ships,
Chinese-type ships:
Names in writing we can't read.

Container ships,
Container ships,
Container ships,
Container ships:
Boxes full of everything that everybody needs;
Chunky ships,
Clunky ships,
Cheeky-little-monkey ships,
Dodging in and out and altering their speed.

Fat
Long
Fast
Slow
(Slow? So slow, her should have been scrapped years ago!).

Cold ships,
Old ships,
New ships, blue new ships –
With natty yellow lifeboats, and shiny stainless fluestacks.

Ships which are blundering,
Ships which go plundering,
Ships full of TNT, nervous when it's thundering.
Ships with sickly sailors chundering:
Too much scotch on an empty tum –
Or too much curry:
Ooh! Phew! Pardon my bum!

A ship that does its training even when it's raining:
A beautiful barquentine
(Wafting scents of linseed varnish, hempen rope, and turpentine).
Boy and girl cadets up there,
Out along the strumming spar,
Struggling with the sails – **BEWARE**!

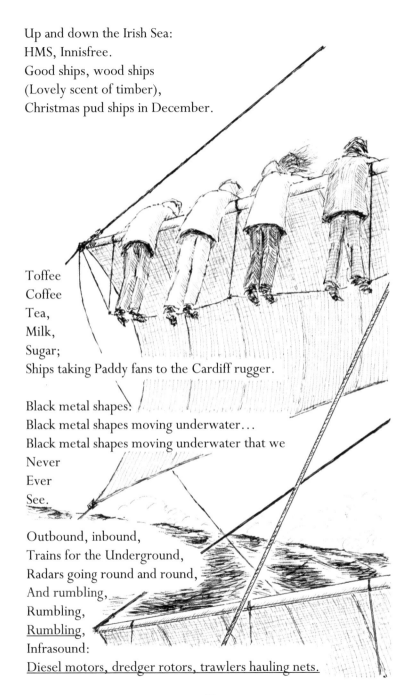

Up and down the Irish Sea:
HMS, Innisfree.
Good ships, wood ships
(Lovely scent of timber),
Christmas pud ships in December.

Toffee
Coffee
Tea,
Milk,
Sugar;
Ships taking Paddy fans to the Cardiff rugger.

Black metal shapes:
Black metal shapes moving underwater…
Black metal shapes moving underwater that we
Never
Ever
See.

Outbound, inbound,
Trains for the Underground,
Radars going round and round,
And rumbling,
Rumbling,
Rumbling,
Infrasound:
Diesel motors, dredger rotors, trawlers hauling nets.

Ships looking frisky, and
Some weighed down with whisky,
Cider, lager, Real Ale,
Guinness, and wine.

All day, all night:
Thick fog/
Sun bright/
Snow white/
Sleet grey/
Rainy day.

Force ten,
Now and then:
So much spray…
Wish that we could see our way!
But mustn't slow down – lose some pay.

Course is good
(Touch wood: it was last time I looked);
But, like us sailors,
Visibility is poor.
Helmsman's squiffy
(Needs more coffee),
The radar's iffy:
Don't know exactly where we are…
…Or anybody else.

Helmsman's squiffy,
Radar's iffy:
Right now,
If someone's bow
Comes out the fog –
It will sink us
In a blooming jiffy!

PEREGRINE

Without warning, from high behind us comes
That unmistakeable edgy call.
We twist round quickly, eyes eager…
But the grey crossbow shape is already a beach away
And, as ever, moving with electricity's ease.

Though a squadron of choughs scrambles from the next headland,
And every bright-billed bird,
Squawking warnings down the coast,
Is immediately jetted far aloft by grass-tugging updraughts,
They're none of them fast enough to intercept the intruder:
By now it's cleared the sector they defend, and the one beyond.

Certainly, gulls can air-slide along the coast for effortless miles:
It's one of their nicer skills,
That knack of gliding into or across the wind.
Indeed, no-one aloft over Wales better understands
The invisible mathematics of shearing air…

Save the slate-sheened falcon, Kills With Speed:
That taloned titanium blade which,
Forged by Nature and honed by Time,
Silently slits our salty winds,
Faster even than the swift.

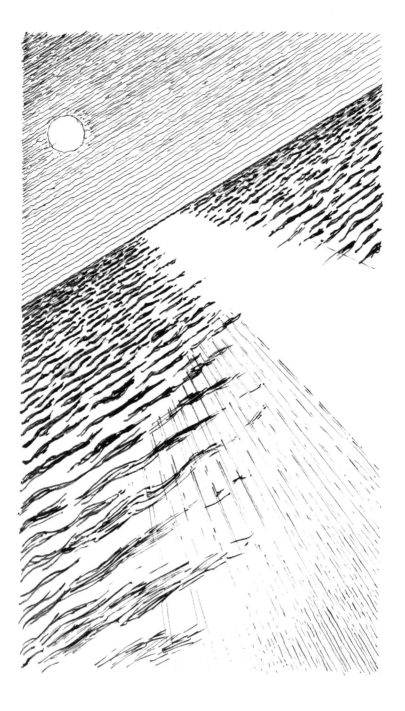

ALL IN THE MOON

All in the moon I swim, and it seems that
The light
Of she who invisibly moves whole oceans
Calls just to me:
'Slip under now, and
Swim inside my brightness!'

Down I dive, and I do;
And I am as silvered
As the under-surface of the sea…
And the peaceful sand
Which sleeps deep below,
Rippled by the rhythm of the last tide.

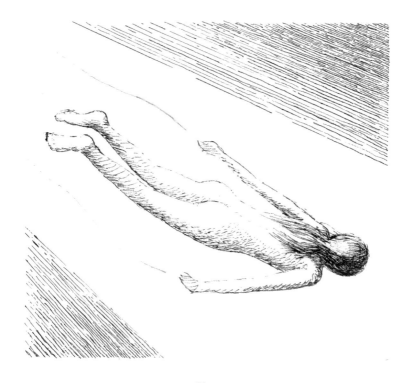

THE DUNE

The dune was great for running down, bare feet flying…
Again and again and again and again, we children, never tiring,
Because those huge springing sand-slope strides
Made us momentarily airborne –
And, thus, we could sort-of know how being an angel felt.

That dune: it seemed shaped especially by God
To catch the beach-heated sea breeze, funnel it upwards,
And send our cotton-and-bamboo kite soaring,
Its silk tail streamers shimmering,
Spinning its bobbin of grass-scented cord.

A natural arena in the dune's midst, hot as Spain at midday,
Was, we girls saw it immediately, Heaven-meant for dancing in.
Chins thrust with Iberian pride, we strutted and pouted
In our plain school cozzies, with plain school towels
Tucked round our plain school waists.
We flicked as best we Cardiff could those MADE IN ENGLAND hems
With flamenco bravado.

And though suncream-slithery fingers
Poorly imitated staccato castanets
We were, every time,
Transported a thousand miles southwards.

The dune's far end was perfect terrain
For belly-crawling commando sorties
Which were essential, tactically, for our **Operation Marram**:
Always, that was the name of any military game.
Off we would snake to recce the imagined gun emplacements
Of an undefined but always Gerry enemy…
Until, one day, our older brother was captivated
By a powder blue gingham bikini, and what it described to him –
Yet perfectly protected from his oh-so invasive eyes.

An untold place within the dune
Was for private lollish downrolls,
Sloth-slowly so sand didn't bother your face…
Just one oveny half-rotation at a time,
Your belly and legs, then back and bottom
In curious love with that skin-pressing fluid heat:
Hot as it was dry as it was glaring white,
Or glaring red to closed eyes;
And inquisitive, ever, as quicksilver.

And always, afterwards…
The dash for, the rush into, the plunge inside
That ungranuling lukewarm late afternoon tide –
Which, we each-other-oggling-underwater girls inwardly knew,
Because it was part of God's knowledge,
Learned all of the dune's secrets
From our silently-gossiping sea-bared skins…
As, breath held sometimes to hurting,
With mermaid fingers
We water-combed our holiday-lustred hair.

AFTERNOON RAIDER

Alerted by suddenly overexcited swallows, I
Stumble up from my weeding kneel and,
Sickle cast aside, guess a sky direction…
This time, luck is with me.

She, a sparrowhawk,
Wings spread atwist with tip feathers asplay and
Sun-caught talons airbraking,
Cuts that hedge gap between crab-apple and ash.
Three hunter's air-strides to corner my lawn and then,
Instantaneously winged aeroplane-rigid to swap velocity for lift,
She clears the twinned hazels.

Now, with dexterity ever wanting comprehension,
A dropping corkscrew turn, side-on to the sky,
Around that ten-year beech before,
Folded up umbrella tight,
Away she bullet-plunges through a blackthorn's badger-tunnel
Into the paddock beyond.

HERE

Days here aren't clock-synchronised:
We swim or sail according to the tides
And, dependent on the weather's disposition,
We walk, tend our growing plots,
Or make our workshops loud places.
Even if we're forced indoors and the light is poor,
Time is never wasted:
Always we can cook or brew in the kitchen
Or, in the snug, read or write –
These latter pastimes with feline company assured, if the fire's lit.

It's true, the taste of air here;
True, too, is the spring-drawn water's flavour.
And truer than at many an anonymously-neighboured elsewhere
Are the feelings most people have for their fellows.
It's fine, the salty rasp-scent of resinous sea-timber being worked;
It's knife-edge white,
The frost-clawed starshine which returns in November –
Meanwhile Earth, ever rolling on,
Already plans perfection of colour
In next year's blooms of primrose, thrift, and scabious.

Whoever thinks us uncultured
Who live by labour, craft, or cultivation
– And of course by strong thought, too –
Let them.

Without understanding
They come to visit,
And pleasurably sneer…

And are all soon gone for good,
Thank God!

A MAP REMEMBERS

Many years ago the humble Dale peninsula played an important part in British history, as confirmed by a bronze plaque displayed beside the coast path near Mill Bay.

This celebratory poem was inspired by a conversation with Jean Thomas, a marvellous lady who dedicated her whole life to education and learning: she had delighted in showing me how the spelling- and sometimes even the sense of local place names varied so much between the maps of one era and those of another.

In our ancestral memory, history sleeps.
Without you feel it, every of us
Keeps within us hidden witness to all years
That went before, whether times of hope or times of fear.

Maps, even maps full modern in design
Cannot help but to recall the earlier times:
The shrines of saints we have forgot today,
And place names old when David knelt to pray.

We look back now past many generations
To when the future of this British nation
By one event was altered suddenly:
The bloody change of Royal dynasty...

Five hundred years ago and more,
Great happenings upon this humble shore:
Close where those rocks divide the breakers' roll,
A Royal bark, from France, makes Welsh land-fall.

Prince Henry Tudor leaps, and then he stands
Upon the golden slope of Mill Bay's sand;
Soon, heading Northward 'gainst the steepening slant,
Declares he to his court "This way is brunt".

And while his armies muster all at Dale,
The retinue proceeds up Snelston's vale;
Past Kestick,
Merrybro',
And Broom Hill,
By Haggardhay descends to cross the rill.

The castle fires no shot,
No challenge calls;
For sympathy's ensconced
Within its walls.

Tho' kingly-blooded, see we now this man
To James the Great give humble kneeling thanks;
For kindly to his ship were sea and weather,
Which out of exile here have him delivered.

And now Prince Tudor asks this of his Lord:
To bless the expedition, and the Cause;
Wish him all safe progress to Haverford
And Eastwards thence, to meet his foe in war.

His foe...

Richard Plantagenet, he wears the English crown,
And thinks the squires of Wales to him bow down;
But, no: the Tudor line they would ensure —
To Henry they have all allegiance swore.

And so our Prince at Townsend meets his troops:
Some thousands, disembarked from Breton sloops.
Knights' horse hoofs make the shores of Gann resound,
And Hal's at home here, crossing Pembroke ground.

The tramp of armed men marching fills the air:
Some folk hide in cellars; some just stare.
Past Pickleridge, past Crabhole onward press
The soldiers, glad of every mile's progress.

The heavy walls of Philbeach dull much sound;
But down the mighty chimney comes that pound:
The Master climbs the roof to watch this sight;
The Mistress calms the child who would take flight.

The Mullock Bridge one Rhys ap Thomas guards:
He's oathed to never let the Tudor pass;
But at a signal, see to where he moves:
Beneath the arch, new loyalty to prove.

And so unhindered Hal our lands doth leave;
Thus onward through the Princedom with good speed.
Dukes, Earls, and yeomen all to him will yield;
Fate, too, rides with the throng to Bosworth Field!

Dale Roade
N
Pykell-Rid
Townfende
DALE
Haggerdhaie
Broomhill
Costell-Beache
Merrie-Borrow
Watt-Wyke
Keffyke
Brynte
Mill B.
S. ANN

SHE'S A TOMBOY!

I envisaged the style of this song as traditional Rock 'n' Roll, typified by **Jailhouse Rock***; but please feel free to sing it any way you choose – or, as with any of the other songs, you may recite it as a poem...*

Provided that you promise to make a lot of noise doing so!

Ginger hair, flaming like a flarestack,
Jumping up and down on the roof of a tin shack,
Piercing eyes like you've never seen,
Handy with a chainsaw, understands machines!
Running round in rigger boots,
Doesn't ever give a shoot,
What her stupid parents think –
Light a fire and raise a stink!
'Cos she's a tomboy, a total, total, tomboy –
A hard-kicking, jeans-ripping, skinny-dipping,
Unexploded bomb boy!

She can cut and she can rivet, she can drill and she can weld;
Instead of wearing dresses, she would rather go to hell.
She's never known to suffer from the Hesitation Blues:
Better run for cover, brother, if you ever light her fuse...
'Cos she's a tomboy, a total, total, tomboy –
A hard-kicking, jeans-ripping, skinny-dipping,
Unexploded bomb boy!

She is light and skinny, but her fists are made of iron;
She runs like a cheetah, she fights like a lion.
Her feet are tough as leather, she loves to go in water;
She climbs like a leopard, and swims like an otter...
She's a tomboy, a total, total, tomboy –
A hard-kicking, jeans-ripping, skinny-dipping,
Unexploded bomb boy!

She could do more damage than a B52,
She'll never, ever, listen to the likes of me and you;
Ain't never cared for discipline, she ain't no Momma's Girl,
But if - she - wanted, she could rule the world,
'Cos she's a tomboy, a total, total, tomboy –
A hard-kicking, jeans-ripping, skinny-dipping,
Unexploded bomb boy!

Please don't ever think you can control this child–
She's ain't one of us – she was born to be wild!
A special sort of kid, and the home that she deserves
Is a thousand acre forest in a wildlife reserve…
'Cos she's a tomboy, a total, total, tomboy –
A hard-kicking, jeans-ripping, skinny-dipping,
Unexploded bomb boy!

THE COASTING TRADE

*This song reflects the mood of **The Slow Train** (Flanders & Swann), and shares its tune (with permission of the Estate of Donald Swann).*

Line breaks are indicated thus: ~

No more will we cast off to sail on the tide in a working sloop;
I will never again need my seaboots, souwester, and oilskin cape.
No more sounding our way to a wharf up a creek
From Neyland to Carew, or Helford to Gweek:
There are no more watches to keep for the coasting trade.

There's help for the railways~
And government spending on better roads –
So you can't make a shilling,~
Sailing with cargo in hundred ton loads.
Whether coal for the lime kilns, or pit props for mines,
Or cobbles of granite for surfacing lanes –
We'll never ship them again in the coasting trade.

At the oil jetties, the turbine tankers sit so big and proud;
Up a small pill a forgotten brig disappears.

The trows of the Severn are all filled with stone~
And are breakwaters now;
The ketches of Devon lie sunk on the shores~
Of the Exe and the Taw…
The harbours are silting, the old skills are lost –
So we're stripping her rigging, and striking her mast:
It's become a thing of the past, the old coasting trade.

Now I must find a new job to support~
Both my children and wife–
But how I will miss them,~
The freedom and peace of the sailing life:
Farewell to the curlews who'd wake us at dawn,
For the race to the mills with the season's first corn…
The men in my family were born to the coasting trade,
To the coasting trade.

MY THINKING TREE

The creak of the trunk as it gently bends;
The lift and dip of the branches' ends;
Pine needles sighing as the wind blows past;
A sweet scent of resin, like a varnished mast…

I'm alone at the top of my Thinking Tree,
Quite a long way up, but I'm safe as safe can be.
It's the loveliest sensation, here, of riding on the breeze –
As if I'm in the crow's nest of a sailing ship at sea.

You've probably guessed: this is my favourite place,
Cut off from every member of the stupid human race.
No always-nagging parents, no pestilential brother;
And nothing electronic: I don't want to be bothered!

Sitting astride a crackle-barked limb
Which is warm as a horse in the strong summer sun,
With my eyes both closed I must rest for a while
Until the frown I was wearing is replaced by a smile.

Then, let me look beyond the woods and meadows too
Past rivers, over hills into that deep mysterious blue…
And when I can clearly see the distant ocean's diamond twinkling
I know that I am ready for some clear, unworried thinking

Of course it's a fierce secret, what I muse about up here
Scrutinising the horizon, and the sky so huge and clear;
But there isn't any question that this brain-time does me good:
I always clamber back down in an optimistic mood.

I know I'm really lucky to have my Thinking Tree;
I hope that you can find a field, or riverbank maybe
Where you can go to be alone, and sort your feelings through:
This world needs more deep thinkers ~
Whose hearts are strong and true!

ADMIRATION

Your eyes taste sweet as apples, when they love;
Your steady breath recalls the gentle sea.
Your touch, just reaching, feels as soft as barley;
Your walk stirs scarce one grass head,
Barely bends the clovers down.

It's such a mystery that one so subtle, one so equally wise,
That one full-roundly kind and always so great of heart
Should choose me as companion
Who is, by comparison, so clumsy…
And, oftentimes, emotionally, unseeing –
Who, though doing their best, gets so much wrong,
Has wronged so many people down the years.

I thank you for your faith in me, shall thank you all my life:
Companion, friend, inspirer; fellow parent, darling wife.

A COASTGUARD'S LOT

Tune: **A Policeman's Lot** (Gilbert & Sullivan, The Pirates of Penzance.)
The chorus' lines are in italics.

1

When the yachtsman isn't idling on his mooring,
   Loads of money!
When the diver isn't hanging round the pub,
   Griffin Inn
They likes to start their engines and go boating,
   Makes you jealous
Taking lots of drink and lots of lovely grub,
   Lovely grub!
When the dinghy sailor's slept off his hangover,
   Too much lager
When the rowing girls have bunked off from their jobs,
   Kate and Gill
They're inclined to venture out upon the oggin
   Lovely evening!
With cans of beer and cheese and onion cobs.
   Can't we go too…?
No! For the watching of the seaways must be done
   Must be done
So a coastguard's lot is not a happy one
   Happy one!

When the trawlerman has fouled his own propellor,
Silly gubber!
When the tanker drags its anchor near the cliffs,
Fast asleep!
When the Navy has forgotten where a rock is,
Where the chart says
It's us they always call on VHF.
How we laugh!
So we have to put on oilskins and wellies
Very fetching
And venture out in rain and snow and fog,
What a drag!
And we always miss a good show on the telly
And our supper!
When a Great White Shark turns out to be a log.
Or a dead sheep!
But still the watching of the seaways must be done
If you say so
So a coastguard's lot is not a happy one
Happy one!

3

Now we've been involved in rescues that were hairy,
Not so funny
Like the ship that hit the rocks when full of gas;
LPG
But there's times we gets a taste of the exotic:
That's more like it!
Once we fished out seven veils and then a lass.
Very pink!
Now the press all ask us, "Isn't it exciting…"
Bloody media!
"…to be there when there's history being made?"
Load of tosh!
But you'll never live it down from your old missus
What a temper!
When for the film crew you embraced the maid.
So did we!
So 'cos the watching of the seaways must be done
All the time
A coastguard's lot is not a happy one
Happy one!

4

Now you're trapped in here, and we've got your attention,
  Stop daydreaming!
So we'd ask you to sit up, and take down notes:
  Safety first!
You must never leave the shore without flotation
  Flares and compass
Even on the shortest trips in little boats!
  Be prepared!
For old Neptune has a nasty sense of humour:
  You can't trust him!
He has such devious tricks tucked up his sleeve;
  Acts of God!
And the sirens he employs to do his bidding
  So alluring!
Will drag you down beneath the briny seas.
  Davy Jones!
AND… Because there's the watching of all you lot to be done,
  Bloody public!
A coastguard's lot is not a happy one!
  NO, IT AINT!

LATE SEPTEMBER

Ice cream continues to sell well;
But the swallows have left.
Still, postcards are put in the shop's outdoor racks
Whenever the weather is fine;
But the swallows have left.
The sea remains warm;
But the swallows have left.

No more excited chatter just outside the kitchen
While I make breakfast;
No more pointless panicking
When I go to the shed for the scythe.
No more cheeky aerobatics around my feet as I
Walk the paddock's perimeter,
Rousing flies from the long grass.

As the bare 'phone wires bear witness,
The swallows departed yesterday,
And I am missing them already –
But at least I have my shed back,
Meaning I can start to sort my firewood uncursed by hirundines.
And now I have no reason not to wash the car;
For, henceforth, it will afterwards stay clean.

THE DEVOUT LONGSHOREMAN

"Longshore" is short for "along the shore". In the USA, a longshoreman does dock work; here, the word is used more loosely, describing anyone who — however occupied — spends much time on the beach, or close by.

In theory, all wood that drifts in should be handed over to Her Majesty's Receiver of Wreck — in theory.

In practice...

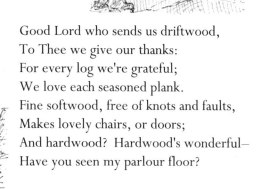

Good Lord who sends us driftwood,
To Thee we give our thanks:
For every log we're grateful;
We love each seasoned plank.
Fine softwood, free of knots and faults,
Makes lovely chairs, or doors;
And hardwood? Hardwood's wonderful–
Have you seen my parlour floor?

To the patron saint of beachcombers
We offer up this prayer:
When a top-notch load of timber comes,
May the Receiver be elsewhere!

GIRL CADETS' HORNPIPE

Advice for any young lady with Grey Funnel Line career aspirations.

Is your hair too long – whether curly, whether straight?
Every time you have a shower, does it get into a state?
Is it frizzy when it dangles? Does it always get in tangles?
'Cos you'll never be a captain if your hair's too long!
It's a long way to the salon where your ship will roam;
And you'll hardly find the time to use your brush and comb:
It is safer to despatch it lest you catch it in a ratchet,
And you'll never be a captain if your hair's too long!

Can you swim damned well, in a flat calm or a swell?
Can you float like a cork just as easily as walk?
Can you wriggle through the water ~
Like the best of Neptune's daughters?
If you want to be a captain, you must swim damned well!
You must never be afraid of jumping in the sea,
For a game of water polo or emergencies;
There's no time for paranoia, just go fast as a destroyer:
If you want to be a captain, you must swim damned well!

Is your cabin neat? Does it never smell of feet?
Are your clothes all nicely folded, and not piled up in a heap?
Is there never insurrection when it's time for an inspection?
If you want to be a captain, keep your cabin neat!
Keep your shoes all clean and polished and in good repair;
Have a nametape firmly sewn in all your underwear;
Don't wash white clothes in with red clothes, ~
And be sure to air your bedclothes:
If you want to be a captain, keep your cabin neat!

Do you eat good stuff? Do you always eat enough,
For a growing sailor who is strong and bright and tough?
Do you nibble at the edges, or get stuck into the veges?
If you want to be a captain, you must eat good stuff!
So it's goodbye to the burger bars and sweetie shops,
And it's hello to the Brussels sprouts and mutton chops –
You'll be glad you always dig in, ~
When you're up there in the rigging:
If you want to be a captain, you must eat good stuff!

Keep your cool, my dears, is the best tip you will hear:
There's no room on board for people paralysed by fear.
You must never, ever panic: just remember the Titanic!
If you want to rise to captain – keep your cool, my dears!
When you're making your decisions, keep a level head:
It's the sailor who is flustered who will end up dead;
So continue with your plannin', even when you're firing cannon:
If you want to rise to captain –
KEEP YOUR COOL, MY DEARS!

95

OCTOBER MORNING: THE OLD WOODEN HUT

The weatherboarding is gale-frayed.
For a septet of decades, the edges of the slats
Have been decaying: they no longer overlap.

We peer between them, and stretch our focus
Beyond the glinting angles and radii of cobweb catenaries
And out, right out, to where the toothy swell
Jostlingly saws along the horizon's joint,
Apprently intent on parting sea from sky.

The locomotive shininess of this collapsing bracken
– Still dark green, but without doubt dying –
Tells us that the dawn's sea mist was heavy:
A West Coast Scot would have said
That today's earlier morning had been *Dreich*.

Then, mist must have coalesced here, its drops lensing
The ocean's inversion – and its every globule
Minutely contributing to the moistening of those
Disappearing edges, softening them for the rasping jaws
Of Autumn's last-chance wasps...

So slowly, those stripy fruit-fed fliers
Are destroying this emptied home:
They create, each building season,
New citadels with those old fibres
In their *perpetuum mobile* of pulping and papermaking.

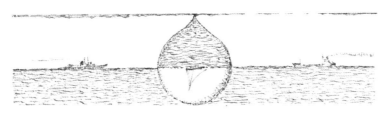

AN EVENING IN EARLY OCTOBER

Not since May has the fire been lit…
Beachcombed last winter,
The summer-dried wood catches quickly
And burns well, with salty orange-flushed flames.

The first steamy fumes condense in the chimney,
Making the stack's cold bricks sweat acid:
Bitter-smelling spit
Drops onto the hissing hearth.

Up top,
The ochre pot becomes wet-mouthed with sullen smoke:
The first damp clouds which grope out
Dew the rim's glaze of sooty tar with glinting black beads.

Bright-eyed jackdaws look on, appalled:
They had thought that they'd found good winter lodgings,
Until then.
Quick to twig the truth,
They take to the air
With much corvine cursing.

I LOVE TO LIVE

I love to live by the wild, wild coast:
The roar of the surf is the sound I like most.
I hear it at night when I get into bed;
As I snuggle down it is all round my head.
Before going to sleep I ask God to care
For sailors and travellers on ships everywhere:
We humans are weak – we cannot control
The power of the waves when the great oceans roll.

I love to live under wild, wild skies:
To watch the great clouds as they go rushing by,
To feel the wind's strength when I'm out in a storm,
To see lightning flash, hear the thunder go BOOM!
As I run for home, I ask God to care
For pilots and passengers up in the air:
We humans are weak – we cannot control
How hard the rain falls, or the strength of a squall.

I love to live near the wild, wild wood –
But I've got a feeling, and it isn't good.
For yellow machines have arrived to make roads,
And very long lorries are queuing for loads.
I must try to stop them, and ask God to care
For forests and jungles, wherever they are.
We humans are strong, and we tend not to think:
A square mile of trees can be gone in a blink.

A STRONG AND STEADY WESTERLY

*It's a slow drive up the coast road between Little Haven and Newgale, and
it can be a frustrating journey when one meets drivers who aren't used to
narrow lanes wedged between high hedge banks...*

Nevertheless, it's a lovely route.

Jackdaws swirl densely
Over Winterton's thickets.
We can't guess what so excites
That vortex of dark cunning,
But of course it may be no more than
Simple wind-joy.

Above Lower Mullock's barn a buzzard hang-glides,
Enough energy in the air today to keep him aloft –
Mind, he can't luff and reef his pinions
With the kestrel's stop-motion accuracy,
And he dips and yaws like a yacht on a snatching bridle
Riding a gallopy chop.

Past sheltered Slate Mill, now, where the brook's silvery ford
Mirrors building work: raw white rafters and bright bare boards.
Just where we top the rise beyond
And our engine can start long-striding,
Freshly blossomed gorse bulges from the bank,
Cauliflower-dense and cleanly bright as just-shipped lemons.

Despite a sun as ever bright as November could dare to expect,
Saint Brides Bay today is gun grey.
It's been turned turbid by so much recent rain –
And hail, as well, indeed, which last night
Sporadically rat-a-tatted our wood stove's metal chimney,
Sometimes outlouding the radio's concert.

Broad Haven's low tide billiard table is not deserted,
Although the half term break ended yesterday.
As usual the local dogs are out,
Morning-walking their people;
And, anyway, this week always seems popular
With folk who have toddlers,
Or children not yet swallowed into school.

Don't think, though, that those little ones aren't learning at all
Out there on the
Bobblehatted sand:
It's evident from their pointy scampers along the tideline that,
With every few question-splashing steps,
Something new is learned.

Great coloured hands, high-stretching to cup the wind,
Tug surf folk northwards and southwards.
Newgale's sky is made garish
By that marriage of ingenuities:
Harnessing of the snaffling air,
And mastery over unreinable waves.

Brawdy's long-empty runway seems especially wrong,
On such a day!
Was there ever better Autumn weather
For sharp bright swept-back wings
To kerosene slicingly up into a visibility of uncountable miles?
But on the old airbase sleeps…

…As does crouching Lower Solva
Which, with the wind in this quarter,
Sends up straight threads
Of blue-dyed smoke
From the dreaming chimneys
Of its weaving lanes.

MISSING YOU

No stove already warm and bright,
When I come in from the garden's dusk;
No vegetables put out, for me to peel for both of us.
No basket by the back door, silently requesting a fill of logs –
Reminding me, also, to ash out,
And hatchet-split some pine for kindling.

No other basket, your Monday one,
Damply heavy with laundry for the line:
Because the grass is dewy, will I boot up and hang it out, please,
While you put the next load on?

No scented palm to rub my head, then bring comforting coffee,
When I forget that low beam, but it doesn't me;
Nobody to loofah my back in the bath or,
Our skins kissing, rinse to a clean squeak
My shampoo-massaged hair.

No happy jealousy
When the cat chooses your lap to purr on;
No bantery crossword-tackling,
While spoon-tinkled cocoa mugs tilt.

No you sleeping alongside,
On winter nights glad to be cuddle-welded close,
Whose last murmur of the day often told me,
'You're warm as a boiler…'
Plus, sometimes, '…and as rumbly, too!'

No waking perfume-rapt, with that elation of
Inbreathing through your hair
Which electrified every morning like a child's Christmas dawn –
No matter that sleet window-slatted, or a choked gutter gagged.

Everything's wrong, because you're not here:
The cat and I, we want you back so badly.
Return soon as you can, my love, my very reason,
My always muse:
With you, this place is Home; without, it's just a house.

A COTSWOLD MEMORY

When I lived up the Frome valley from Stroud, walks from my cottage
could take one either along beside the river and the Thames & Severn
canal, hearing the trains on the embankment above straining up the steep
incline, or through the beech woods, so differently beautiful in each season
— or beyond the houses behind mine, and out across the high wold…

On I walked, and on I walked, and on I walked,
And on; and on the drizzle soddened.
And on its bringing westerly sang,
Saddening every 'phone wire.

But I nevertheless was a happy lad,
For all that it weathered;
Happy, though my boots squeaked with saturation,
Though my coat's proofing had surrendered
To that siegeing precipitation,
And more unsheltered tarmac miles lay between me and home.

Happy because, in the moment between
That unknown library-girl
(As I imagined her, although more chance she worked in a bank)
Stepping from the hiss-stopped Stroud bus
At the lonely pub back there,
And launching the umbrella which would huddle her down
That sycamore-weaving side lane
To her unseen cottage…

In that moment

She took the trouble to notice me,
And smile encouragement –
And did that smile convey, too, a country-dweller's envy
For the windswept freedom of my wet afternoon now dusking?

INDIAN SUMMER

Extra days of mellow,
Gifted by Luck:
Only by outdooring our lives
Can we love them
As we should.

FOX

Making every wind-twist advantageous,
Across the field's skyline,
Fur-sleeked fluidity
With the evening's gleam upon it:
A fast-trotting fox's hurried undulation,
With a snout kept ground-intent –
Until it intersects the downwind of me...

Ears cocking forward and shaping into scoops
As he snaps his head round,
In the moment it takes Fox to stop,
His owl-fast eyes have already fixed me
Like a destroyer's rangefinder...

The space between us no detriment,
He has me for nose-flaring interrogation.
He so well knows my species; his scenting stare tells
My sex, my health – probably my fitness, too.
He knows what I've just eaten,
That I wear wool and something wax-waterproofed,
Where I've been walking, and more besides...
But he can't tell my mind.

However, as he doesn't detect gun oil,
Which is the smell of farmers' anger,
I am thus not a threat, in his hope.

So, head holding me in its cunning-calibrated sights
To measure my reaction,
Fox starts to move, gently,
Making to resume his original vector…

Only when I am seen to stay still,
Am confirmed as not initiating a closing manoeuvre –
Only then does Fox set his head forward again,
And strike on at the previous speed.
Ever wary, though,
He swings towards the West:
To sooner brow the rise, thus faster deny me line of sight…
Just in case.

YOU EVERYTHING ARE

I don't think I will ever meet
Another girl e'en half as sweet –
Nor half as strong, nor half as wise,
Nor half as lively in the eyes!

Your every word doth me inspire,
Your every movement lights a fire;
I never knew 'twas you I sought, but,
Now we've met, the past means nought.

Come live with me, you darling girl:
In my world's oyster, you're the pearl!
Or say the word, and I'll be gone –
Though still my love endure full strong.

RORRIM LRIG

I pull the plug, step from the bath,
Then quickly swish it neat;
Towel-wrapped, I scoot off to my room:
Can't wait to feel its heat!

Shiver-hastened, see me scorch inside;
A back-kick slams the door –
But then I'm frozen statue-still as my towel drops to the floor:
I'm looking at another girl I never saw before!

Because while it's me, there in my mirror,
Hair wet, cheeks russet red,
Who stands and frowns, so quizzical
By that familiar bed...

Well – it's me, but then it isn't me,
Eyes peering clear and grey:
I'm seeming, now, to see myself
In a very different way!

I move a little closer, to look a great deal harder
At that girl who's there reflected:
Mother's colour, hair like her father's...

She's just like me, but then she's not
'Cos I don't feel I'm so tall –
And as for those new-starting curves...
I don't know those at all!

I stand there, very thoughtful,
The mirror's message clear:
I'm going to look quite different
By this time next year!

MY POETRY

My poetry does honestly seem to write itself.
So you could say, I suppose,
That it's only *my* poetry
Because I'm the person who,
Whenever new lines suddenly occur to themselves,
Is always on hand, ready to write them down –
Wherever I happen to be at the time,
And whatever I'm doing.

WHY I TALK TO TOM MALONEY

I hope that lots of people will hear this poem, and get the message.
  Jess is, thank Goodness, an imaginary character.

A time comes every day when I fly into a rage,
Or I lose control and then I cry and cry;
My Mum, she's really great, she doesn't blame it on my age –
You see, there is a different reason why.

What I like to do when I've badly got the blues
Is to get my wellyboots and yellow mac,
And I go off down the lane to see my good old mate again –
Who always listens, never answers back.

His name is Tom Maloney – did you guess that he's a pony?
He isn't super handsome, but who cares?
Once I've given him his apple, my brain it tries to grapple
With what's happened to my best friend: it's unbearably unfair.

Tom Maloney, kind old pony, understands why I feel lonely:
I'm really, really missing my friend Jess:
We've been close for lots of years, but now her future is unclear;
For Jess stays on in hospital, and I'm completely lost.

When we saw her last weekend, they said ~
'She might be on the mend;'
But she lies completely still, and never moves.
I try telling her my news, won a race and got new shoes;
But she lies completely still, and never moves.

She lies completely still, and never moves;
There are wires and beeping screens and lots of tubes;
She can't see, she doesn't hear, and you know what we all fear:
That Death is going to win this fight, and Jess is going to lose.

Coming back from grooming Tom in the early evening gloom,
In yellow coats we shone a torch, held hands, and sang a song.
When we heard that car come zooming, ~
We stepped back to leave more room;
But the way it took the corner was all wrong.

Until I die, I won't forget the moment that it hit:
How I tried to pull Jess up that muddy bank!
But I fell back on the grass and, with a thump, she left my grasp;
Something struck my head, and everything went blank...

And perhaps it's just as well, 'cos it would have been such hell,
That waiting for the helpers to arrive;
And what would I have said, then, to that wretched Mr Joad...?
The man who ran down Jess, because his car came off the road.

He lived a busy life, and worked hard so that his wife
And his children had a big and comfy home;
Now his family has gone, and Jessie's heart just stumbles on,
Because he drove and used a mobile 'phone.

Because he drove and used a mobile 'phone
She lies completely still, and never moves.
She can't see, she doesn't hear, and you know what we all fear –
Because he drove and used a mobile 'phone.

It doesn't matter what they drive, people threaten other lives
Every time that they pick up their mobile 'phone:
Think of Jessie, badly maimed, and of Joad, who is to blame –
Because he drove and used a mobile 'phone.

In the car with any grown-up, if they go to pick the 'phone up,
You **know** what you must ask them, every time:
Is there *ever* a good reason, night or day, in any season,
To put at risk a precious life like Jessie's, yours, or mine?

GULLS

They may be the dustbins of the skies,
Puffin-thugging bully birds,
Salmonella-spreading scavengers
Of gutters near chipshops,
Rubbish tips,
And sewer outfalls –

But each posesses a divine knowledge of the air,
Riding with a surfing ace's sensitivity
Its invisible cusps and currents.
Fearlessly they encounter the ambush of updraughts;
To them, it seems, slicing shears and wing-wrenching vortices
Which would terrify any sane pilot
Are all just part of the fun of flying.

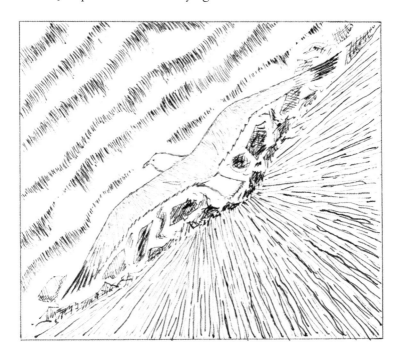

SAVED FROM THE FIRE

The new winter has begun digging, out there under the bay:
On that cobbled tideline at The Sands' south end,
Where everything of wreck accumulates,
Today I find not more time-thinned ship ribs,
Nor another plank galleried by bloated sea-worm bores,
But a small timber complexity.

A rust-pickled palm-fitting shape,
Middled by an irrefutably man-made disc,
Its still accurate circumference grooved of old:
Fused into one by at least a buried century, I'm holding
The cheek and sheave of a ship's pulley block –
Whose bearing insert is, I suspect,
Of *lignum vitae*: the Wood Of Life.

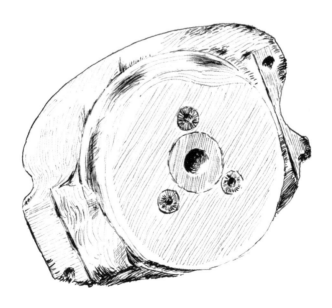

Not that that fact could prevent its death,
The vessel whose rigging once lofted this block!
Peering seawards against ice-blue wind and brittle December sun,
I picture her foundering:
Masts toppling from a reef-burst hull,
Their rock-shredded canvases ripping free;
Waterlogged corpses and drowned cordage
Submitting to salt-rot and myriad scavenging teeth.

I must take home this piece of unknown truth:
Better to share enjoyment of its mystery with speculating friends,
Than leave it for the next ignorant fag lighter…
Often, so often, sea-history's offered hints
Are annulled by beach bonfires of such pointlessness,
They're lit on balmy days.

SLANT ME THE SUN

Slant me the Sun down low,
Low as you please.
Midwinter it, if you will;
Or, more freezily, acutely angle its rays
For uncaring early February…
If it shines well, unhazed,
And the waves don't overfiercely break –
Into them, even under them, my skin shall gladly go!

WINTER CROSSING

BASH!, CRASH!, SMASH!, goes the up-down sea,
Hammering the bows of the push-pushing ferry;
Rocking and a-rolling with her top-heavy hull,
Trying to keep to time in the teeth of the gale.

Splash!, Wish!, Wash!, go the bridge window wipers
And the captain and the helmsman think it's all a jolly laugh;
Wim!, Wom!, round goes the arm of the radar,
Peering through the rain to see the other ships out there.

Rev!, Roar!, Rev!, go her unhappy Diesels,
Fit to bust their bolts when her props come out of water;
Wheesh!, Sheesh!, Wheesh!, go the mighty turbochargers,
Boosting up the air pressure: so much fuel to burn!

Curse, cuss, and worse, go the chefs in the galley
As the soups start a-slopping and the teapots overspill;
Curse, cuss, and worse, 'cos they cooked such lovely food –
But no-one comes to buy it: they're all feeling ill.

Shoup!, Wherp!, PUKE!, go the green-faced passengers,
Vomiting in basins and borking into lavs;
Burp!, Borp!, BEAUGH! go their wrenching empty stomachs:
They feel so flipping rotten, they wish that they were dead.

On it goes, and on it goes, and on it goes, and on,
Lurching, dropping, slamming all across the Irish Sea:
Nobody believes that the ship has stabilisers –
Or if it has, they can't be working: oh, what wretched misery….!

FOOP!, FOOP!, FOOP!, goes the siren on the funnel:
At last we've reached Rosslare, and we're backing to our berth.
'THANK THE LORD!' cry the passengers with one voice,
Can't wait to get their feet back down on good old solid earth.

Out go the cars and in drive the lorries,
Going home to Germany, or France, or even Spain.
Gobble, Guggle, Guzzle, in pumps oil for the Diesels,
Re-filling all the fuel tanks: that was such a thirsty run!

Hiss!, Buzz!, Skrak!, go the messages by radio:
Captain talks to Port Control, and Port Control to ship.
Zip!, Zop!, Zip!, bridge computer printing weather maps;
Then, totting up the passengers, it pushes out a list.

FOOP! from the funnel and SPLASH!, there go the ropes;
CLANG! rings the telegraph and, from the Diesels, gradually,
Building up, BLURALURRALURRALUMMM!! So,
SPLURSH!, the propellors thrust; and we're off a-flipping-gain!

LAPWING

Lapwing swims air scoopily –
Same way that Turtle flies water.

KEEPING WARM

Wood heats you four times over: when you cut the tree down; when you saw it up; when you split the logs... Finally, when you burn them!

This song should work well with many an old folk tune — or how about inventing your own music to sing it to?

The weather, this February, is bitterly cold:
Sharp aches in the bones of the folk who are old.
My children come to me with the basket for the logs;
They say, 'Daddy, please fill it!'; I wink at the dog.
And I say...

Chorus
If it's warmth that you seek,
If it's heat you desire —
There are things you must do
Before you sit by the fire!

In their boots and their coats and with hats on their heads,
In the spinney they find an old ash-tree, quite dead;
While I smoke a pipe, and the dog can relax,
The children chop down that tree, using my axe.
(Chorus)

And after more work, with its twigs now all gone,
With long ropes they drag that tree all the way home;
I stand back for safety, and so does the dog,
And we watch as they saw the trunk up into logs.
(Chorus)

The children split all the logs up with the axe,
And then in the woodshed the fuel they can stack…
I say to them, 'Now you may have a good blaze!'
They reply, 'We're too hot now!', and stay out to play.
(Chorus)

Outside it's now snowing, but the young folk still play;
Inside, by my fire, I reflect on the day.
When winter is biting, the things I like most
Are ale which is well mulled, and hot buttered toast!
(Chorus)

You like stories with twists in; I try not to fail –
So here comes another, to finish this tale:
Burning unseasoned wood is a countryman's crime…
That ash tree will warm us in three years' time!
(Chorus)

WINTER STORM

Many Dale houses enjoy superb views of the Bay, and far beyond; having studied a wild sea from my friends' upstairs sitting room window...

Beaufort eight, and gusting ten: wind enough, all right.
The side gate succumbs, bursting its gale-worried hasp
And detonating against the wall with a land-mine's flat BANG!
So out we rush, to staunch its self-destruction
With prop, wedge, and concrete block.

Overhead, our electricity lines dance loopily,
Skipping copper ropes;
Meanwhile above the paddock, taut as cheese wires,
Howling high tension cables
Strain against wetted insulators crackling spitefully.
Fortunately, deep-rooted in its terra firma,
Their transformer pole is steadfast.

The ancient imaginations of our children
Hear no mere vibrations in the air: their ears are convinced
Of a heavily panting sky, and baying squalls.
Lurking this darkening cloud-scabbed gloom
Could be, they know,
Thor's Norse wolves: huge, and mercilessly smallbody-hungry –
Who wrench, relentlessly vocal, against His restraining chains.

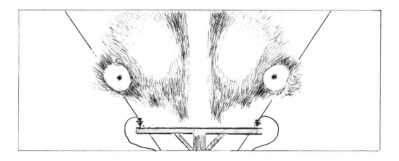

Quick, get back indoors –
The snug's chimney is spitting sparks!
Redly reverberating in its inglenook, the wood-burner
Has become a greedily-breathing Bessemer furnace,
Hellishly bent on melting itself.

Though hanky-lagged fingers slam-shut
Top and bottom damper levers,
Still it drags all the air it needs, and more,
Between the firedoor's slats of heat-crazed glass,
Or through the gap around the ashpan's rattling hatch…
And, 'Damn!', now the casting's got another crack.

Atop our stove, steam-full as a locomotive
And shrieking like a non-stop passing Swindon near the ton,
The spray-spitting kettle kicks and stamps against the side-rails
As each spattered drop, after dervishing a fizzy hotplate dance,
Skitters beneath its restless bottom and petulantly explodes.

To placate the seething back-boiler and silence rabbling pipes,
An involuntary bath is run for the children –
Who, inevitably, beg not to be ordered into it.

Sawdusted, leafmoulded, burred, and crumpet-crumbed,
They'd rather stay wedged into the window seat,
Taking breath-held turns with the binoculars,
Lest they miss the Biggest Wave So Far
Cala-BASH! itself to lathery bits
On Great Castle Head's red grindstones.

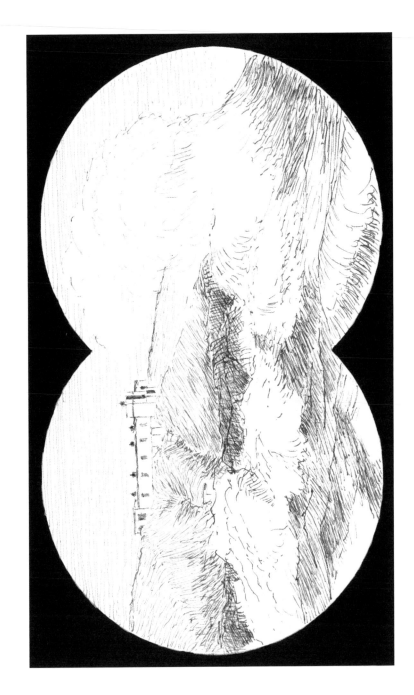

Yet, once they've wrangled promises about what'll be for supper,
Their upstairs galumphs disappear with heart-hitting giggles
Into the floral-scented fog…
Now's our chance to swing the shutters out, click the clips…
And, with ears cringing, scree the brass-ringed curtains closed.

But the storm is not so easily excluded:
Shifty and unsettled, those drapes are.
Incoming salvoes of force-full air
Which shake the window sashes and gun-rattle the shutters
Belly them out…
Only grudgingly do they answer to gravity, and drop back down.

Too soon for one begun to snooze, the girls return from Bathland
Soap-sweet and downily wrapped.
Handed soup in mugs, with towels discarded
They make the ovened hearth their home:
Two Copenhagen mermaids, side by side on a spark-singed rug.

In the flames' gleam they glow like new-cast bronze as,
With the static-crackling brush, in turn they play at styling hair –
And don't tackle the untangling of each other's knots,
As Mother had negotiated.

But we forgive them trespasses such as these:
We were just as headstrong; we were equally excitable.
We, like them, caught storm fevers;
Indeed, how we wish that we still could feel the elemental frisson
With that eyebright intensity.

The wildness of this night will, we know,
Make instant sleep impossible in that attic bedroom –
With rain gravelling its skylight, and every winding punch
That the Sou'Wester lands upon the slates
Making the joist-joints groaningly complain.

And so this will be both the best and worst of nights:
They'll start with nursery tales, the stories ever sillier;
Then, the storm's infection will turn the themes
First to piracy, next murder,
Last to ghosts – and not the placid ones.

But on will go the game of whisper tennis; and, girls,
You will fabricate between you stories so shocking,
Yet ever worsening…
Until, though toasty-warm, you're both
Too goosy with apprehension
Either to open your eyes, except under the covers –
Or to close them at all, for fear of horrid sleep.

Both, by then, so scared, that neither of you can possibly face
The night of mares alone,
Bigger Sis must spring: two hurried scalding-cold steps
Across a canyon of haunted lino.
Squashing in next to quaking Tich,
She'll murmur calming words until the breathing's even;
Then fall asleep herself, with arms encircling
Her Digestive-scented fairy-haired hot water bottle of a sibling.

Now, from the leaf-swirled porch, feline scratches and yowls.
We run to snatch the latch –
But keep the chain on, fearing for a squall.
With the dark pressure of a weir-pent night river
Sinisterly sluice-sliding from between bulwark beams…
Our rain-blackened tabby extrudes out from the gap,
And flies firewards like a loosened barrel bung.

Soaking paws cheetah across quarry tiles, leaving gleaming prints:
Puss hastens, weather-cursing, to the top of the log box.
Where, sung rhymes of sympathy by the heat-soaking girls,
He starts his preening,
And soon begins to steam.

On he will clean, and on he will steam
– Unless proffered milk intervenes –
Soliloquently purring beside his roaring iron friend,
Until unto his coat's restored
The springy nap and oaty flavour
Of a proper, itchily-warm Witney blanket.

Only then will he recce where to sleep;
And, if he deigns,
He'll honour a human
By selecting their lap as the theatre stage
For his tempested enactment of
Paw-twitching hunter's dreams.

"JUST A TUG"

When people look out from the shore,
To see what ships are there…

Some have to clock the tankers, know how many thousand tons
Of oil that they can carry, be sure which is the biggest 'un.
They crave those ship statistics: so many metres long…
And as for how deep in the sea – oh, they love to check that one!

Meanwhile others best like warships,
Low-hulled and sleek, all grey:
'Can they really go as fast as *that*?'
Oh, how great to see one rip along,
Flat out, her bow high-sheeting spray, one day!

Some folk "collect" container ships; and some, the cruising liners.
The latter, getting ever bigger…
Just like those five-course diners
Who wobble to their restaurants with the appetites of miners.

And nearly everyone loves tall ships,
Precious survivors from the Age of Sail.
So graceful, no pollution – but don't forget the broken arms,
The bloody nails, the frostbite, men lost overboard in gales…
That was such tough travail
For the men who served before the mast
In our maritime past.

But there's one sort of ship that nearly everyone ignores –
My sort. You see, I'm a tug.
People overlook me because I'm not very big
– Compared with the ships I have to handle –
And I'm painted a dull colour,
Unlike those ooh-look-at-me gas tankers…

But without my efforts, all your
LNG carriers, cruise liners, freighters, container ships…
NONE OF THEM COULD ENTER OR LEAVE THIS PORT.

Without me pushing and pulling,
Leading, swinging, and braking them,
Fighting the winds and currents which would otherwise
Ram them into a jetty or force them onto a mudbank,
High and dry 'til the next tide –
Without me, they'd be scuppered.

So, when you eat your supper tonight with, I bet,
Lots of food in it from overseas,
Remember me and my mates,
Who stayed up very late
To see those ships with all those goodies aboard
Safely into Felixstowe, Tilbury, Southampton, Avonmouth,
Or Dublin. Or Sydney. Or Singapore…
You get the idea.

So perhaps in future you'll show more respect,
And never again sweep your binoculars quickly past
That admittedly boring but nevertheless essential silhouette,
Sneering,
"Just a tug".

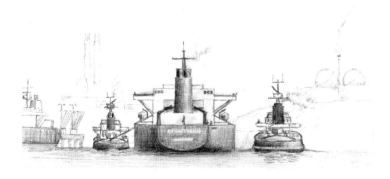

I AM THE CHRISTMAS SEA

I wake to a bright calm dawn.
Hearing the ocean calling across silent frost-furred fields,
Sure that those sunrise colours promise a perfect morning,
I dress hurriedly.

They aren't up yet; this suits the plan:
I make preparations while the kettle boils.
Bringing them tea in bed,
I ask about visiting The Sands –
Nicely, but persuasively too.
'…And, if we go early, while the tide's lowest,
We might have the beach to ourselves!'
Two miles of wild shore.

I make us a fast breakfast: just juice, crumpets, and bananas;
As soon as I'm done, out I dash
To start Dad's engine and scrape his icy screen.

It smiles on us, the luck we've made for ourselves:
When I halt, breath jumpy and heart pumpy,
At that point on the path
Where you can at last see the whole strand…

There's not a footprint anywhere
On that sun-stared sand;
And, just as my ears had promised me they would,
The waves crumping ashore look huge fun,
Without being frightening.

After sprinting to the tideline, I apparently welly about aimlessly
Along the foamy edge,
Whilst actually assuring myself that the sun's warm enough
And the waves aren't too strong.
Decided, I deliberately hang back,
Pretending that limpets suddenly interest me…

And, 'Yes!', off they head southwards:
Attracted by the high tide wrack line, they assume I'll catch up.
But I've been checking which barnacly bluff
Makes the best changing place –
And *there* is where I now leave my
Backpack, coat, boots, socks…
Everything.

No hesitation: straight into the shining sea, at the splashing run –
And the playful water rushing puppyishly to meet me
Is so superbly crashy,
Such massive and immediate fun,
I never give its temperature a thought.

Knowing I must do it soon, I choose: 'THIS IS THE ONE!'
A breaker bigger than me –
Meaning that if, as it arrives, I don't do a huge leap
To arc over its crest, I'll *have to* dive…
Air ingasped, I spear myself under.

Opening eyes immediately…
Oh, the beauty of winter waves, each a green-glowing gale-gust
Sweeping across the sun-dappled sand
In a silver-spiralled dance of bubbles!

I start to swim out deeper, head twisting about so I miss nothing,
Determined to stay submerged as long as I possibly can:
There's so much to delight me down here, so much to remember!

Eventually, breath all used, I can't any more ignore my lungs:
I kick myself up a sparkling sunbeam
And burst gasping into a swaying world of snow-bright fizz.

Bobbing about in it,
Ducking giggling through each glass-clear rushing crest,
I start to cackle with Christmas glee because, I'm sure of it,
So absolutely sure that I shout it to the blue-hung gulls above,
THIS IS MY BEST SWIM EVER!!!'

Why?
Because today, in this joyous tumult,
I understand as I never have before
That I was born a Nature-creature.

Indeed, I feel so at one with these winter waves, it's as if
I didn't just then run into the water from the land,
But actually swam shorewards from a secret sea-home,
Far out there and down so deep,
To play here where the swell meets the sand.

Could that land-life have been a dream?
Was I brought up in this water-world?
So it seems, the way that
Each time I leap with a wave at just the right moment,
Like a powerful playmate it familiarly grasps my body…

And that lovely strength I trust sluices me forward,
Transformed into a whooping bobsleigh of a sea-sprite
As I go hurtling down another steep foam-slope,
Thrilled all over by the tickling prickles of myriad bubblebursts.

I've become part of these winter waters:
Sharing so much joy
As together we play ancient but evergreen games,
I am the Christmas Sea.

WHEREVER I GO

This school leavers' song is inspired by memories of former pupils who were educated at Dale: what fortunate children! An early summer theme, yes – but the message of farewell is appropriate for the last piece in this book.

Wherever I go when I am grown older,
Wherever I live and wherever I roam,
I'll never forget the fields of my childhood,
I'll never forget this dear place which is home.

Whatever my work when I am grown older,
I hope that I'll always have time to play sports:
I'll never forget school games and athletics,
And summers of swimming, and bike-rides, and boats.

Whenever I'm tired, whenever forgetful,
When those they call clever all say I'm a fool,
I still will be proud to say where I come from,
I'll always be glad that I went to this school.

Whatever I know when I am grown older,
Of trouble and crisis, disaster and war,
I'll think of the times when lessons seemed so long,
And then I will wish that we could have learnt more.

Whoever I meet when I start exploring
The countries and oceans that make up the world –
I'll never forget the friends of my childhood:
So lucky to know all those boys and those girls!

Whenever I hear of a ship on a home run,
Whenever I see a train heading far West,
I always will want to be travelling back then,
I always will yearn for the land I know best.

Musical score: Page 150

Where do poems come from?

It greatly helps the imagination if you've grown up in a family fond of poetry, singing, listening to tales, and not just telling old stories but dreaming up entirely new ones.

From my first arriving in this wonderful world, my mother and three sisters entertained me with nursery rhymes. We tuned in, daily, to *Listen with Mother*; I was always read a bedtime story. As our family's cars never had radios, on long journeys we'd either spin out long circular yarns, or we children sang – with Dad often joining in. My earlier school years were full of poems, songs, and hymns (which are poems of a special sort); I always enjoyed English lessons.

My ears, ever delighted by rhythm, rhyme, and word-play; for my older eyes, the fun of crosswords. Classical music, down the years; plus Rock, Blues, folk and roots, jazz… And, constantly, the influence of Shakespeare.

Nevertheless, there were decades of only writing engineering reports and personal letters; so, what decided me to have a serious try at composing poems and songs…?

The coast, sky, and land of Pembrokeshire had long been inspiring me as an artist: they seem to want to be painted. Also, I slowly realised, the world hereabouts is full of good words and thoughts, **if** you can tune your senses in: sea and wind can whisper or shout; water beats rhythms; trees and stones sing, albeit differently to birds and seals; and such telling ballets are discernible when animals and people act or indeed interact.

Sensations, emotions, and impressions: a cornucopia, there for the harvesting, all year round.

About capturing poems

Like picture possibilities, poems pop up without warning. So, I must always carry with me the wherewithal to record both interesting views and ideas for word-dances… Wherever I go!

CCCP

OLD RUSSIAN FREIGHTER
F Minor

Metronome 120 BPM   *Rolling Along*

Up and down en- or- mous swells on the At- lan- tic O- cean, our

cap- tain's full of vod- ka, and we've got a cra- zy bo- sun. Our

ship is real- ly an- cient, and we spend each day in fe- ar, and

all our lives de- pend up- on a one- eyed en- gi- nee- er. Not

one of us is | on this ship be- | cause we vol- un- | tee- ered; but

we all know much | bet- ter than to | ar- gue with su- | pe- riors!

You might have expected a suggestion to play this song sadly; but seafarers are typically stoical, in other words they cope with whatever happens without getting too upset. Also, as sailors tend to be sentimental, I like to think that the crew of this old vessel would have been fondly proud of the way that she kept plodding across the oceans of the world for them like a faithful horse, never complaining as long as her appetite for coal was satisfied, and her engine got its regular doses of oil and grease…

…In any case, Russians will tell you that something about their national spirit makes them quite enjoy feeling melancholy.

Do make full use of those pauses!

The hammer and sickle emblems on old Soviet Russia's merchant navy ensign represented Industry and Agriculture.

OLD RUSSIAN FREIGHTER (BARYNYA VERSION)
F Minor

Metronome 120 BPM   *Stompily*

Up and down en- or- mous swells on the At- lan- tic O- cean, our

cap- tain's full of vod- ka, and we've got a cra- zy bo- sun. Our

ship is real- ly an- cient, and we spend each day in fe- ar, and

all our lives de- pend up- on a one- eyed en- gi- nee- er. Not

one of us is | on this ship be-|cause we vol- un- | tee- ered; but

we all know much | bet- ter than to | ar- gue with su- | pe- riors!

This time I have tried to make the music sound more Russian, by having the left hand imitate a stompable balalaika accompaniment.

This should firstly help us to imagine our way into the ship's engine room, where we see the up and down and round and round of the reciprocating steam engine.

There's still every reason to make good use of the pause marks: the poor struggling engine surely slows down, heaving the ship up every steep wave.

So – what's a Barynya? As I understand it, the Cossack style of dance where you start slowly and get gradually faster. Let's picture the sailors, partying in the fo'c'sle despite the storm outside, with the oil lamps swinging to the roll of the ship and their mugs of drink sliding about on the tables.

If you can get people to have a go, the question is... Will someone brave be trying to sing the words ever more quickly, as your fingers race over the keys?

BLUEBELLS
C Major

Metronome 83 BPM   *Brightly*

Blue-bells dan-cing in the breeze, blue-bells dan- cing by the sea,

Such a sight to meet the eye, so much blue be- neath the sky

Blue- bells make the air so sweet, in the wild or in the street;

It's the per-fume we love best: scent of blue- bells from the West!

Instead of playing this piece brightly, you could go further and deliver it joyously or indeed dancingly.

And, of course, dancingly is the only suitable way if someone's jigging about as you are playing!

VIKING RAIDERS
E Minor

Metronome 85 BPM   *Urgent*

This must be performed with a strong beat: imagining the Vikings at sea, we hear a tireless rhythm which paces the oar-strokes steadily as the longship surges along; advancing on land, surely they sword-thwack shields to confuse and terrify their victims.

I'M A CRONK!
A Minor

Metronome 95 BPM   *Proudly*

I'm a Cronk!, I'm a Cronk!, I'm a ra- ven, a

ve- ry big, ve- ry black bird; my de-

mea- nour is dra- mat- ic and I'm good at aer- o- bat- ics; but

yes I must ad- mit, my song is not the best you've heard. I'm a

Like buzzards, ravens are proud birds; and they're intelligent: their 'Cronk!' is far more eloquent than the crow's 'Caw!' As for their sense of humour – they are not just very good at aerobatics, they clearly have great fun, tumbling about in the air-swirls which brow a windy cliff.

Do pay attention to the pauses: don't rush this song!

I'M A CRONK! VERSE 5
A Minor

Metronome 95 BPM

Proudly

I'm a Cronk!, I'm a Cronk!, I'm a ra- ven, a

cen- tu- ry's no- thing to me! I've seen

Cle- o- pa- tra's war- ships and the Vi- kings in their Norse ships… And

I'll still be here when there's no- one left to sail the seas! I'm a

…And off the raven flies, back to their patrolling of the cliffs. It's quite a calm day, and for ages we can hear their call echoing flatly from rock faces, boomingly when they cross curved coves which are shaped like amphitheatres.

Quite a calm day; but the big bird still gets enough lift from the onshore updraught to be able to glide on outstretched wings.

THE END OF THE VOYAGE
C Major

Metronome 65 BPM

Thoughtfully

Now here we are, back in our home port safe and well; the an- chor's

down, and we have furled all of the sails - the sun is

set- ting, and the sky turns deep- est blue - there is no

watch to keep for cap- tain or for crew. We have sailed

far, in wa- ters wide and wild - seen ves- sels

lost, to death been re- con- ciled - hot were the

tro- pics, and so strange the Nor- thern Lights: such me- mor-

ies, we have en- ough to last a life.

There are quite a few pauses, aren't there? They're inviting you to play or sing this piece with much feeling.

You can surely imagine how a travel-wearied mariner, telling you about their adventures long into the evening, hesitates from time to time as particular memories become suddenly vivid again in their mind's eye – so, try to convey that blend of deep reflection and a passion for discovery.

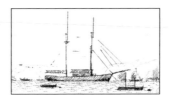

THE END OF THE VOYAGE (ARPEGGIO VERSION)
C Major

Metronome 65 BPM   *Thoughtfully*

Now here we are, back in our home port safe and well; the an-chor's

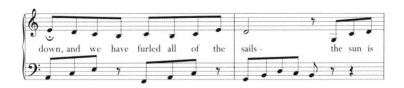

down, and we have furled all of the sails - the sun is

set- ting, and the sky turns deep- est blue - there is no

watch to keep for cap- tain or for crew. We have sailed

far, in wa-ters wide and wild- seen ves-sels

lost, to death been re-con- ciled- hot were the

tro-pics, and so strange the Nor-thern Lights: such me-mor-

ies, we have en-ough to last a life.

Although I have printed the lyrics to Verse 1 on these two pages, this version of the music should work very well as a song without words. The right hand tells the sailors's stories, modulating between pride, excitement, nostalgia, and sadness; meanwhile the left hand, which shouldn't ever play stridently, provides the background sound: the gentle lapping of the sheltered bay's wavelets against the hull of the resting vessel.

WHEREVER I GO
D Major

Metronome 45 BPM   *With spirit*

Where-ev-er I go when I am grown old-er, where-

ev-er I live and where-ev-er I roam, I'll

ne-ver for-get the fields of my child-hood, I'll

ne-ver for-get this dear place which is home.

So many different feelings, when we finally leave junior school. While the words reflect on what we will miss, they also acknowledge that, thanks to our teachers and friendships made with fellow pupils, we're ready to go further and learn more.

WHEREVER I GO (CELLO VERSION)
D Major

Metronome 45 BPM   *Nostalgically*

Where- ev- er I go when I am grown old- er, where-
ev- er I live and where- ev- er I roam, I'll
ne- ver for- get the fields of my child- hood, I'll
ne- ver for- get this dear place which is home.

Similarly to the Arpeggio version of *The End Of The Voyage*, this should work very well as a song without words.

With both instruments playing in the bass register, the music probably wants to be given a more reflective mood.

INDEX

Poems & Songs

Musical scores

This book is dedicated to the memory
of my youngest sister,
who never got to properly know the Pembrokeshire coast
while she was with us.

It comforts me
to imagine Diana finding her own way
to the Marloes peninsula…

and falling completely in love with it.

Suggestions for adding colour

This book is printed on high quality paper with a slight "tooth"; with well-pointed ordinary coloured or watercolour pencils you should be able to achieve quite strong effects.

I've also done tests using watercolour and acrylic paints: working dryly, you should get good results without any "cockling".

In my felt pen experiments, colours didn't bleed through; however, being familiar with more traditional techniques, I wasn't confident about achieving sufficient subtlety – and sketches like this one, *Girl in a Gale,* do call for a subtle approach...

If you would like to see more examples of my paintings and drawings, and some photographs, please visit

www.asummerbreak.co.uk

On this website you can also find out a bit more about the writing side of my life; but, I must confess, I'm not one for frequently posting progress reports!

There's plenty of useful and interesting information about Marloes and St Brides on the official website:

www.marloes.org.uk

SPRINGBOARD PRESS, ISBN 978-0-9928774-0-8

July 1980

With just hours to go, Sophy's holiday plans are scuppered.
So — must she stay at home all summer…?
Not if she takes up a spur-of-the-moment offer.

The beautiful West Wales coast gives this English girl a feeling of freedom she has never known before and, quickly making new friends, she soon finds herself riding remarkable horses in situations she could never have imagined.

As her true spirit emerges, Sophy discovers much about the wider world, and herself — and everything points to a future very different from the one she and those she loves might have expected, had she never come to Pembrokeshire.

Christopher Jessop writes poetically; sometimes his carefully crafted style is quite complex. He hopes that readers of any age will find this a rewarding book, with much in it to entertain, amuse and intrigue them.

"The narrative pace is sustained admirably throughout the sequence of adventures, and Sophy is an appealing heroine with the right blend of vulnerability and tomboy courage."

Pembrokeshire Life magazine